Stocks on the Move

Beating the Market with Hedge Fund Momentum Strategies

Andreas F. Clenow

Registered Office: Equilateral Capital Management GmbH, Talacker 50, 8001 Zurich, Switzerland

For details of editorial policies and information for how to apply for permission to reuse the copyright material in this book please see our really neat website at www.StocksOnTheMove.net.

ISBN: 1511466146

ISBN-13: 978-1511466141

In memory of my brother, Mathias Clenow.

January 9, 1973 to June 30, 2015.

It's been a lot of fun writing this book and I had plenty of help from some great people. The support, inspiration, comments and suggestions have been invaluable in completing the book. In no particular order, I'd like to especially thank Frederick Barnard, Julian Cohen, Philippe Hänggi, Jon Boorman, Riccardo Ronco, Didier Abbato, Patrick Tan, Tom Rollinger, Erk Subasi, Kathryn Kaminksi, Raphael Rutz, Michael Bennett, Francois Lucas, Yves Balcer, Mebane Faber, Nigol Koulajian, Greg Morris, Nitin Gupta, John Grover, Ales Veselka, Jani Talikka, Nick Radge, Thomas Hackl and Larisa Sascenkova.

1
Preface

This is an entire book about a single trading strategy which can be summarized with the simple statement 'buy stocks that move up'. The idea is very simple and it's certainly not anything new. As a concept, this is old news. What this book tries to offer is a clear and systematic way of managing a portfolio of momentum stocks.

The ideas presented here are based on my own experience as a quantitative hedge fund manager. I've been managing institutional portfolios based on this concept, as well as other strategies, for the past decade or so. The simple ideas are usually the ones that stand the test of time. That doesn't necessarily mean that it's simple to implement them, but the underlying concept should preferably be very simple. In this case, it's really simple. A stock that has been moving up strongly for a while is likely to continue doing so a little bit longer. That's the core idea. The rest is details.

I wrote a book a few years ago based on another type of trading strategy that I've been using for many years. That book was called *Following the Trend* and the entire book was about a very simple trend following strategy for the futures market. When writing that book, I was quite sure that few would even notice it and I expected mixed reviews at best. The main concern that I expected would be raised was that the book was essentially a 300 page research paper. That's absolutely valid. That's exactly what that book was.

Much to my surprise, no one raised that concern. I didn't hear it once. Instead, my book took off in a way that surprised both me and my publisher. After two years my publisher tells me that I, against all odds, ended up in the top 5% of finance book authors. It was a fun ride and I learnt a lot along the way.

Momentum Investing

This book is about systematic equity momentum. Momentum investing is a rational way to manage your money, as long as you've got a protection from bear markets in place. The problem is that it's complicated to construct a solid set of rules for how to pick your stocks, when to buy them, how much to buy, when to sell etc. If you like to construct realistic simulations of your trading strategies before deploying them, which I really do recommend, momentum strategies are very complex to model.

It's a simple concept, but constructing a solid simulation is very difficult. The data is both expensive and difficult to use. You need to take cash dividends, historical index membership, delisted stocks and other issues into account. Then you need a simulation platform powerful enough to handle the vast amount of data needed. I've already done that work for you. I'll present the result to you and my analysis of it.

Of course, I'll give you enough details so that those who do have access to the necessary tools and data can verify my work. If I didn't do that, I wouldn't have much credibility. Anyone can claim anything if it can't be verified.

What I'll do is to present a complete set of rules for managing a stock momentum portfolio. It has performed very well in the past and it's very likely to continue to do so. Feel free to use it.

Why Write a Book?

This question always comes up. Why would I write a book and reveal my super-secret methods to the world? The question itself is based in a common misunderstanding that is often found in the retail trading community. I'm not revealing anything that hurts me or my business. A trading methodology like this doesn't work that way.

There are many multi-billion dollar players in the equity momentum game. They trade according to similar principles that I outline in this book. Not the same, but similar. They have large research staff and they have massive budgets. There's nothing in this book that these firms don't know or can figure out on their own. So who should I keep these secrets from?

If a few thousand people read this book and start managing their own money according to these ideas, that's great. It certainly wouldn't destroy the profitability or take away money from me. It just won't make a difference, considering how much money is already managed in momentum strategies.

If anything, I'm hoping that some who read this don't have the time or patience to implement the strategy, and instead lets my asset management firm manage their money. I'm happy to explain how everything works, but many people still need a professional investment manager.

So why am I writing a book? First, it's quite fun. I enjoy writing and I very much enjoyed the contact I had with countless readers after my first book. Second, there's nothing really to lose. No secrets to give away. Hopefully my ideas are slightly better than what others have published, but we're dealing in details. Third, there's the potential of finding new interesting clients for the actual business, asset management.

And if you thought that I write for the glorious revenues you get from book sales, you've obviously never written a book.

2
The Problem with Mutual Funds

Almost everyone in the developed world has an ownership stake in a mutual fund. Even if you didn't actively buy into any mutual fund, your pension fund is most likely invested in some of these vehicles. Mutual funds seem like a logical solution and they have been hailed by governments, universities and banks as the perfect solution for individuals to participate in the equity markets.

Before you buy into a mutual fund, you should be fully aware of what it really is and how it works. Most people are not familiar with what a mutual fund tries to achieve and how it goes about it. Even more importantly, you should be familiar with how mutual funds have performed in the past. After all, asset management is a highly measurable business and it's quite easy to compare and analyze how investment products actually performed.

While the idea of collective investment schemes is quite old, the mutual fund industry as we know it has only been around since the 80's. The overall idea is to allow for anyone to participate in the general stock market, even with smaller amounts in the simplest possible way. Of course you could participate in the markets by simply buying a basket of stocks, but you'd quickly realize a few practical problems with that. If you're looking at an index such as the S&P 500, like the return and would like to replicate it, you'd have to buy into 500 stock positions. Well, some have such small weights in the index that you could probably get a close enough replication by just buying half of the 500 member stocks. But you'd have to keep track of the weights and the membership changes and actively manage your portfolio to match the index. If you don't, you wouldn't get the same return as the index. Perhaps more, perhaps less, but not the same.

And what if you would like to invest $100 a month for long term saving? It wouldn't be possible as you can't buy fractions of a share. Even if you want to follow the Dow Jones Industrial Average with only 30 stocks, you can't buy them with for such small amounts. Even if you could, you'd have to handle weight rebalances and all the other hassle that most people simple don't want to do, and would not be able to do.

Enter mutual funds, the savior of the poor people and the democratizer of financial markets. Each fund aims to follow a specific and predefined index, and as a small investor you can simply place your $100 with the fund and it will be pooled with everyone else's money and invested to replicate the index. Almost.

As the mutual fund is measured against a specific index, they are relative investments. This means that their job is not to make money for their investors. Go on, read that last sentence one more time. A mutual fund is tasked with attempting to beat a specific index. If that index loses money, the job of the mutual fund manager is to lose slightly less money than the index. In a bull market, his job is to make slightly more than the index. So far fair enough, as long as you're aware of this.

A core concept in mutual fund world is tracking error budget. It's not like a mutual fund manager can do whatever he likes to beat the index. Far from it. Tracking error is a measurement of how much the returns of a fund is deviating from the index. The daily returns for the fund are measured against the daily returns of the index. The allowed tracking error, or tracking error budget, is normally very small. The fund simply is not allowed to deviate much from the index.

Mutually Assured Destruction

What a mutual fund actually does is to take almost all the money in the fund and allocate it in-line with the index. If a stock has a weight of 5.2% in the index, you buy somewhere between 5% and 5.4%. There's very little leeway for the mutual fund manager to impose his or his bank's investment views. They can at times make slightly larger deviations from the index, but bear in mind that this can be very dangerous.

There's an old expression in the business that governs much institutional investment behavior. *"No one ever got fired for buying IBM."* What this means is, that if you do what everyone else did, you don't risk anything personally. If you lose, everyone lost and you won't get blamed. On the other hand, if you made your own independent decision and bought what you thought was best, ending up losing the same amount, you might very well get fired or at least receive blame. The safest course of action, in particular if you have a comfortable job, is to do as everyone else does.

The result is that we have a giant mutual fund business where everyone does the same thing.

Perhaps it doesn't sound so bad. After all, if they invest in-line with the index, you should get what you wanted, right? No, not so fast. There are bills to be paid too. A decent mutual fund manager makes seven figures a year. The bank will take a management fee, custodian fee, administration fee etc. A mutual fund will of course do all trading with the investment banking department of the same bank that issues the fund, and there's no incentive to get those fees down. There are many different ways to siphon money out of mutual funds and that's a reason why banks love them. They are very profitable.

High fees aren't necessarily a problem, as long as the performance is there. For this to happen, the fund needs to do much better than the index, so that fees can be paid and the investor still receives better than index performance. Given the enormous success of the mutual fund industry, surely they provide strong long term returns and show clear value to their customers, right?

It's a good thing there are people whose job it is to keep track of these things. Let's consult the *S&P Indices Versus Active Funds Scorecard* (SPIVA). They're easily accessible and freely available on the internet at (https://us.spindices.com/resource-center/thought-leadership/spiva/).

Take a look at Table 2-1. After you had a look at it, I'll explain the numbers in the columns. They might not be what you think they are.

Table 2-1 - Mutual Funds versus Benchmark Indexes 2013, End of year
SPIVA report[1]

Fund Category	Comparison Index	One Year (%)	Three Years (%)	Five Years (%)
All Domestic Equity Funds	S&P Composite 1500	46.05	77.53	60.93
All Large-Cap Funds	S&P 500	55.80	79.95	72.72
All Mid-Cap Funds	S&P MidCap 400	38.97	74.00	77.71
All Small-Cap Funds	S&P SmallCap 600	68.09	87.32	66.77
All Multi-Cap Funds	S&P Composite 1500	52.84	80.38	71.74
Large-Cap Growth Funds	S&P 500 Growth	42.63	79.78	66.67
Large-Cap Core Funds	S&P 500	57.74	80.56	79.39
Large-Cap Value Funds	S&P 500 Value	66.56	76.75	70.26
Mid-Cap Growth Funds	S&P MidCap 400 Growth	36.72	79.37	86.19
Mid-Cap Core Funds	S&P MidCap 400	43.48	67.27	83.94
Mid-Cap Value Funds	S&P MidCap 400 Value	45.33	73.97	67.14
Small-Cap Growth Funds	S&P SmallCap 600 Growth	55.61	86.10	69.60
Small-Cap Core Funds	S&P SmallCap 600	77.70	91.10	74.73
Small-Cap Value Funds	S&P SmallCap 600 Value	78.99	88.00	60.74
Multi-Cap Growth	S&P	38.14	86.54	68.56

[1] Source: S&P Dow Jones Indices, CRSP. For periods ended Dec. 31, 2013. Outperformance is based upon equal weighted fund counts. All index returns used are total returns.

Funds	Composite 1500 Growth			
Multi-Cap Core Funds	S&P Composite 1500	62.74	84.51	77.15
Multi-Cap Value Funds	S&P Composite 1500 Value	49.21	70.68	67.98
Real Estate Funds	S&P U.S. Real Estate Investment Trust	50.00	86.71	80.28

The numbers in the columns show the percentage of funds that failed to beat their benchmarks. Yes, the amount that failed at the one thing they are tasked to do. In the past three years 77.53% of all US mutual funds failed to do their job. Take a look over the table and you'll see that an overwhelming percentage of funds fail on three and five year horizons, and for some over 90%. There's a few numbers lower than 50% on one year, showing that any given year can be a bit of luck while no one performs in the long run.

You might think that this is a particular period where the funds were struggling for some reason. Sadly, no. Every year the report looks more or less like this. They're all available on the SPIVA site, and you can go back in history and compare. What you'll find is that the mutual fund industry is a very consistent failure. That is, from the point of view of the investor. The banks are still making good money.

It's important to understand that the failure to perform is not necessarily the fault of the mutual fund manager. He is forced to allocate almost all capital in-line with the index. He can overweight stocks he likes and underweight those he doesn't like. He can hold a little cash from time to time when he's bearish. There are some tools for him to impact performance, but not enough to overcome the fee hurdles. Remember that he starts off every year in the red, fighting to make back the fees. I don't envy his job. It must be very frustrating. Until the pay check comes in.

Exchange Traded Funds

The idea of exchange traded funds is brilliant. In its original shape they were simply a logical extension of the idea behind mutual funds. With the mutual funds, the general public gained access to the broad markets. They could suddenly achieve a broad diversification and participate in the equity indexes without having large investment amounts. They also didn't need to care about the individual investment decisions as this was handled by the mutual fund manager. But as we've seen, mutual fund managers don't perform as advertised.

ETFs offer a simple solution. The idea is to have a computer manage the fund with the mission to replicate the index exactly. The money in the ETF is distributed to all the stocks in the index it's supposed to track at the exact weightings of the index itself. No deviation, no delays, very low fees, very low costs all around. The result is a vehicle which tracks the index extremely closely.

If you really want to buy the index, buy a passive ETF. That's how you get the index. A key point that I want to raise in this book however, is that buying the index might not be very attractive. It's certainly more attractive to buy a passive S&P 500 ETF than to buy an active mutual fund with that index as benchmark of course.

The original ETFs were all passive index trackers. This is a great concept. What you need to be careful with though is the growing number of structured products that are being packaged as ETFs.

There's a large amount of highly dangerous and deceptive structured derivatives out there, marketed as regular old ETFs. Before you trade an ETF, look into what it really is. Never trust the name of an ETF.

Avoid any sort of enhanced ETF. Avoid any short ETF. Actually, avoid any ETF that doesn't explicitly track a specified index.

Just as a simple example, take something like a short ETF. If you buy a short ETF on the S&P 500, you'd expect to get the inverse performance. If you'd buy a double short ETF on the same index, you'd expect a double inverse performance.

That's true, but only for a single day. See, in order for these funds to be able to offer the exact inverse performance in a single day, they need to be rebalanced daily. If you've got a background in options, you already know where this is heading.

Compare the long term price development of a regular S&P 500 ETF, a short ETF and a double short ETF on the same index. Figure 2-1 shows how the short ETFs tend to fall all the time, except in times of very extreme, short term negative moves in the index.

What you need to understand with short ETFs is that you're trading gamma, not delta. Option traders should have already seen this coming. What this means is that the short and double short ETFs are much more sensitive to change in volatility than to directional change in price. When you buy these short ETFs, you're really putting on a short volatility position.

In all fairness, it has to work like this. If you want to match the inverse performance on a single day, this will be the effect. The problem is that it's not exactly explained to people who trade these things, thinking that they can get inverse performance over a week, a month or a year.

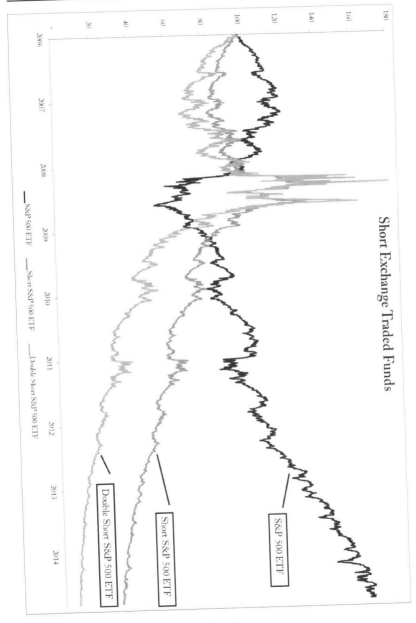

Figure 2-1 Short Exchange Traded Funds

Here's the simple explanation. Start with the index at 100. The first day, the index drops by 10%. Now the index is at 90, the short ETF is at 110 and the double short at 120. Great for the short ETFs. The next day, the index moves back to 100, gaining 11%. Would you expect your short ETFs to be back to where they started? The short ETF, losing 11% of 110, is down to 97.8. The double short loses 22% of 120, down to 93.3.

Repeat this game for a while and it looks like Figure 2-2. The index in that example keeps going sideways, up a little, down a little, but in the end sideways. The short ETF under those circumstances would keep moving down. The double short would move down fast.

The short ETFs is a very obvious example of bad ETFs. They're misleading and can easily cause losses if you're not familiar with structured derivatives. There are many more of these sorts of disguised derivatives in the ETF world.

Exchange traded funds are a great idea, as long as they're straight up vanilla index trackers. Be very careful with any other type of ETF.

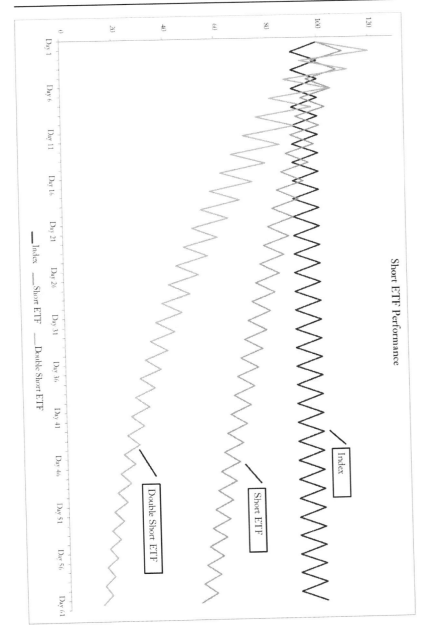

Figure 2-2 Short ETF Performance

3
Equities is the Most Difficult Asset Class

Many investors are drawn to stocks because it seems like the easiest asset class. We all know, more or less, what a company is and what the shares in them mean. It's easier to relate to than commodity prices, bond yields or foreign currencies.

Most people trade companies that they understand. You go to Starbucks for your morning coffee and understand how their business works. You like your new neat iPhone and buy Apple stocks. This is of course an illusion. Your experience with Starbucks coffee or Apple iPhones is not really helpful for predicting future stock prices. It only seems like it, after the fact.

This is an illusion that it's very easy to be fooled by. When you look at the names of publicly traded companies and associate your own experiences with them, it's easy to get influenced by this. If you like their products, you feel that the share price should rightfully move up. If you think that they're outdated, out of fashion or have a flawed product, you feel that the price should be falling soon. Most likely, these ideas are not helpful in trading the stock in question.

It's very easy to look back at a larger price move and think that it was so obvious that this should have happened. Perhaps you look at the dramatic rise in the Microsoft prices in the 90s and say that it's so obvious that they would have dominated not only the software business but the whole stock market. After all, these are the makers of the wonderful operating system DOS and the brand new add-on GUI Windows. Even if you for some reason didn't spend your 90's evenings constantly re-optimizing the extended memory usage though config.sys and autoexec.bat, you would have noticed that there really were no viable contenders around. This was, in retrospect, as clear as it gets. And yet, it was very far from clear at the time. Sure, in the generally prevailing insanity at the time, everyone threw money at any tech stock like there was no tomorrow. But the people buying Microsoft were generally the same that bought Worldcom, Global Crossing, AOL and many other companies that went belly-up in a spectacular fashion. It just looks obvious when it's too late to act.

Quite often companies with great products and seemingly great strategies perform poorly in the stock market. Equally often it's the other way around, with insane sounding concepts skyrocketing. Again, wait until after the stock has moved enough to make headlines, and now it seems so obvious to everyone why it all happened. There's an old expression that everyone's a Monday morning quarterback. Now, as a European I don't really know what a quarterback does, but it doesn't seem like something you're supposed be doing on Monday mornings.

There are certainly people who are very good at fundamental analysis of companies and industries. They're experts in figuring out what will happen in the long run and usually go into extreme details in their analyses. This is a very difficult game and it goes a lot deeper than liking or not liking products. These analysts are often specialized on just one sector or even a few stocks. They follow every detail and analyze every row of their income and balance sheets. It's a perfectly valid approach to the financial markets, given sufficiently hard work of course, but it's a full time profession in itself and not what this book is about.

A very similar illusion is the belief that you have an advantage in trading the stock of the company you work for. It would seem to most people as if their inside knowledge of the company helps them understand the market and achieve an edge in trading. Unless you're part of the top management team or the board of directors, this is simply not the case. Even if you're top management or a non-executive director, it's doubtful that you have any advantage more than at special situations such as just before an important announcement. Those special situations are of course illegal to trade on, generally speaking.

In fact, buying the stock of the company you work for is irrational. First, you don't have any sort of advantage in trading it compared to any other random stock out there. If it worked that way, the employees of any publicly traded company would make more money on trading than on their salaries. It's just an illusion. But even worse, you'd be compounding your existing risk in a single company. Yes, you've already got a risk exposure against the company you work for. If they do poorly, you might get fired. If they do well, you might get a raise and a promotion. By purchasing the stock, you're just increasing your risk against the same entity, without any rational reason for doing so.

Peer Pressure

The equity world gives you the impression that you have endless possibilities. There are thousands and thousands of stocks to be traded. These represent companies doing business in any imaginable business sector. You've got industrial conglomerates, telecom operators, pharmaceutical companies, gold mining operations, internet firms, oil explorers, you name it. The business areas are so extremely different that it would be logical to assume that the share prices will move very independent of each other.

The problem is that they don't. Yes, you've got thousands and thousands of stocks to choose from, but when it matters they will all behave like reindeers. What? The whole sheep metaphor is overdone. I'm Scandinavian, trust me on the reindeers.

In normal market conditions, stocks can appear reasonably independent. When we have a bull market, most stocks go up but good stocks go up much more. Most stocks have a quite high correlation to the overall equity index during bull markets and even if you've got a large portfolio of stocks, you'll be highly dependent on the overall market. When the index advances, so will most of your stocks. And vice versa of course.

In a bear market, this quite high correlation between stocks suddenly approach one at terminal velocity. When the markets suddenly tank, there's no place to hide. Everything takes a hit at the same time. Then when the overall market rebounds and makes a sharp bear market rally, all the stocks turn up on the same day. This destroys the very idea behind diversification. What you're now holding is essentially varying amounts of beta.

This is the single trickiest part with equity strategies. If you're trading all asset classes at the same time, you could fairly easily design a mechanism for diversification. After all, corn, oil, Yen and stocks have very little in common and usually move quite independent of each other. But if you're just trading stocks, you have no such luxury.

The lack of diversification in equities is a factor that it's critical to be aware of. For equity strategies, you will always have a substantial beta position. The more stocks you hold, the closer your strategy will resemble the index. This is important, but not necessarily a problem, as long as you're very aware of it and design your strategies with this in mind. Taking beta risk deliberately doesn't have to be a bad thing. But you do have to be aware of it, and make sure that you don't hold beta when the market is turning sour.

Survivors

The S&P 500 Index is a momentum index. So is the NASDAQ 100, the Dow Jones Industrial, the Russell and most other equity indexes. If you think about it for a while, you'll realize that equity indexes are essentially very long term momentum strategies.

Of course the word 'momentum' is not part of the official Standard and Poor's index methodology. But market capitalization is.

For the S&P 500 Index, in order for a stock to be considered for inclusion, it has to be very liquid, listed on the NYSE or NASDAQ and must have a market capitalization of over 5.3 billion dollars. Market capitalization is simply the theoretical value of the company. You get this by multiplying the number of shares outstanding with the current stock price. The implication of this should be obvious. The reason that a stock is part of the index is that it had a strong price development in the past. When a stock leaves the index, it's usually because it had poor price performance and dropped below the market cap requirement. This makes the S&P 500 Index, and most other indexes, momentum strategies to some degree.

When you look at a long term chart of such an index, you're looking at a momentum strategy. Strong performers are included, poor performers are not. A company can do poorly for a while, but if it keeps losing it will be excluded from the index. As it keeps going down after that, the index itself is not impacted. What you see therefore in the index is very similar to a momentum stock picking strategy.

This all means that the indexes make the equity markets seem better than they really were.

It also creates an illusion of being able to get so called ten-baggers. That expression refers to a stock that increases in value tenfold after you buy it. That's 1,000%. If you look at a stock in the S&P Index and go far enough back in time, you may start regretting not buying it ten years ago. The problem is of course that this stock wasn't in the index then. It's only in the index now because it had an amazing ten years. You probably wouldn't even have heard of the stock ten years ago. Even if you did, it was probably a high risk small cap stock in a sea of other high risk small caps.

When developing and simulating trading strategies, it is of absolutely critical importance that you take this into account.

Let say you're developing a trading model that buys stocks under certain circumstances. Perhaps you buy when they break out of a range, perhaps you buy when they're oversold, it really doesn't matter here. If you program this approach into a simulation platform and test on the current S&P 500 constituent stocks for the past twenty years, it will most certainly look great. After all, the strategy buys stocks from a basket that we know had great advances.

What you need to do is to use a realistic stock universe. A good way to do this is to test on all stocks in an index, such as the S&P 500, but taking historical index constituents into account. You would need to make your simulation platform aware of the historical index composition on any given day. That way, for each day back in time, the simulation would only consider stocks that were actually part of the index on that day. This is a way to eliminate or at least drastically reduce survivorship bias.

A key part of this approach is that you must also include delisted stocks. Many stocks that were traded ten years ago are no longer listed. Perhaps they went bankrupt or perhaps they merged into other companies. The reason doesn't matter, but the important point is that your simulation must be given as realistic parameters as possible.

Most of the delisted stocks had terrible performance. If you don't include them in your simulations, you'll get overly optimistic results. When you then start trading, you'll find out the hard way that reality can be very different from simulations.

Divide and Conquer

There are all sorts of corporate actions that may affect the shares of a company. Most of them are fairly straight forward and easy to adjust for. These are usually adjusted for automatically in practically all data sources. A split for instance, is automatically back adjusted for, so that no artificial gap is introduced. This is all good and well. The real problem however is with cash dividends.

Most time series sources available to the general public ignore dividends. Odds are that most stock charts you've ever seen, and perhaps even all, completely disregard dividends. Even the default charts in expensive market data platforms for professional finance people disregard dividends.

Normally all charts are adjusted for splits and similar corporate actions. If they weren't you would see it quite easily. Just look at the 2014 split in Apple for a very obvious example. In June that year, Apple did a 7:1 split. That means that the price is suddenly one seventh, or 14.286% of what it was the previous day, but in return you'll suddenly have seven times as many shares in your portfolio. The share price closed on June 6, 2014 at $645.87. On the following Monday, the stock opened at 92.72. This represents a dramatic change in numbers, but it's really a non-event.

Splits really have no impact on anything but they can serve as a neat little marketing trick. It's a statement from the company that the stock price has risen so much, that it's become too expensive for people to buy. That's of course not entirely correct, as the price level of the stock itself is not a measure of how expensive or cheap the company is. If you compared two identical companies, with equal number of shares outstanding as well as identical fundamentals and outlook, the share price itself would have at least some relevance.

While a split is a non-event and has no analytical value, it does impact the time series of the stock. In the Apple case, if you don't make any adjustments, you'll get a chart that was moving at around 650 and then suddenly plunged down and lost 85% in a day. It would appear as if there was a major loss for shareholders, and that was obviously not the case.

The way to adjust this is to recalculate the whole series back in time. In case of a 7:1 split, all prices back in history for this stock prior to the split, must be multiplied by 0.142857. As you can see in Figure 3-1, the unadjusted series makes no sense. There was no 85% loss in the summer of 2014 and the time-series shouldn't have a gap there. Don't worry; this job is done automatically by practically all market data providers, even the free internet sources.

When it comes to dividends, the logic is very similar. In order to get a correct picture of the actual financial development of a share price, you need to adjust all series back in time. While a split is usually at least by a factor of 0.5, the adjustments for dividends are much smaller. The standard practice when it comes to adjusting for dividends is to assume that the cash received was immediately reinvested in the same share. This method allows us to easily calculate an adjustment factor and adjust all price series back in time.

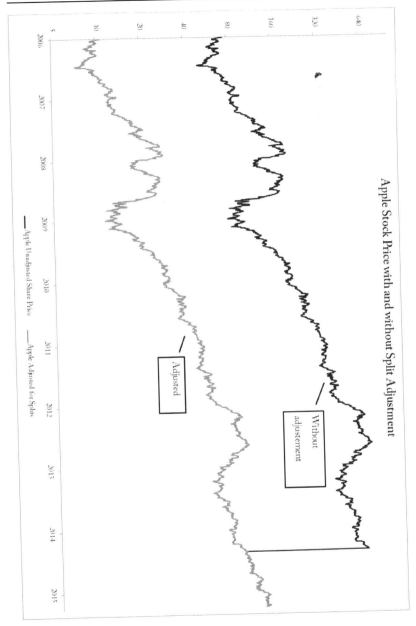

Figure 3-1 Apple share price, without and without split adjustment

Again, don't worry too much about the practical details. It's useful to understand the general logic and the benefits from these adjustments, but it's unrealistic to attempt to do this work on your own. If you plan on running simulations or doing other analysis of longer term stock time series, it would be advisable to buy total return data. This expression refers to data that has been adjusted for everything, from splits to dividends to anything else that might have affected the investor over time.

Figure 3-2 shows AT&T since 1998. One line shows you a time-series adjusted only for splits and other corporate actions, as it would be displayed by default in most market data systems. The other shows you the real development, including dividends adjustment. The first series, which most people would call the normal price chart, would tell you that an investor lost 7% if he bought in 1998 and held until 2015. The problem is that this is very far from the truth. This is a high yielding stock, paying large dividends. The actual result of buying in 1998 would be that you doubled your money by 2015, assuming reinvested dividends.

You may wonder why we assume that dividends are reinvested. Well, because any way you cut it, you'll have to make some assumption about what happens to that cash, and that assumption will inevitably end up to be wrong. Assuming reinvestments is the standard method, it makes logical sense and it makes for useful adjustment figures.

You could assume that the cash does nothing, but that's not likely either. That would imply that you get dividends and put the cash under the mattress. Perhaps we could assume that the cash goes into so called risk free deposits, or is invested in the index. Either way, as you see, we're going to have to make some assumption about what happens with the cash. Reinvesting it means that our entire initial cash purchase stays with the share price, just as it would have if there were no dividends to begin with. It therefore shows a more valid time series of the value development of the company.

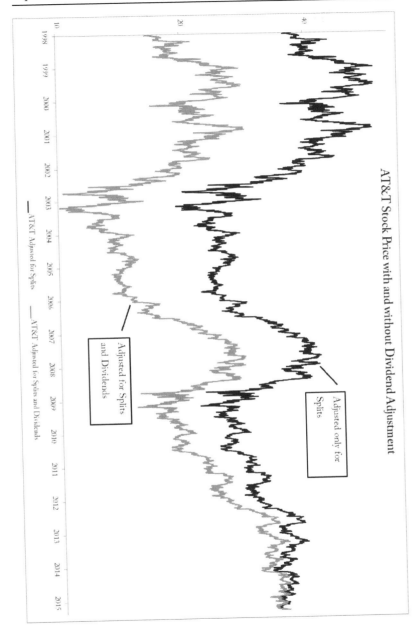

Figure 3-2 AT&T with and without dividend adjustment

The examples shown here are on the extreme side and were deliberately chosen to make a point. Observant readers probably wonder if this really matter so much in normal day to day stock trading and investment decisions. For some type of strategies and methods, it probably doesn't matter that much. As long as you're on a short enough time horizon, and don't happen to trade during a split or dividend event of course.

But it does matter to the type of long term momentum approach that this book is concerned with. There are two problems that come from disregarding these adjustments. The first is about simulations and the second about stock picking.

When developing a trading methodology, it's common to construct a mathematical model and make a realistic simulation of the approach. Without doing so, you're flying blind. You may have a very logical theory about the market, but if you haven't tested its historical validity, you don't really know to expect when you go live.

If your simulation is performed on unadjusted price data, or more likely on price data adjusted only for splits and not for dividends, the returns over time will be very far from reality. Every time a dividend is paid, it looks as if you got hit with a loss, which of course wasn't the case. Perhaps you've got a great methodology, but you could end up discarding it as the simulation shows worse results than it should.

The larger problem is with stock ranking and selection. If you would make a ranking of the stocks that performed the best in the past year, any stock that paid a dividend would get pushed down the list. A company may be on a roll, constantly increasing its profits and rapidly expanding, but since it's paying a dividend it won't show up on your ranking screens.

Without taking dividends into account, you may end up selecting inferior stocks. If you're taking your portfolio selection seriously, and if you're still reading I can only surmise that you do, then you really should look into getting a total return data source.

Choice of Index

For the purposes of this book, the equity market will be represented by the Standard and Poor's 500 Index. It's a broad index of large American stocks and serves well as a general benchmark for the health of the US markets.

Picking an index is more important than it might seem. The index is your benchmark. It doesn't mean that you have to track the index, but it's a yardstick to measure your performance against. If you're not beating the index, you're not doing a very good job. The choice of index also helps you define your scope. There are thousands of stocks to choose from only in the US. Having many stocks available can be a good thing, to a point. It often helps though, if you limit yourself to the members of one, or potentially several indexes. It gives you a defined scope to work from and it's particularly useful in simulating your strategy. If you don't have a clearly defined scope, it's difficult to make realistic assumptions about what stocks you would have considered ten years ago. It's a classic fallacy to look at some stock that just made a thousand percent return in the past ten years, assuming that you would have even heard about it before it started its run.

There's a very good reason why I didn't pick the Dow Jones Industrial Average as the index of choice. Actually, there are several reasons not to choose this index. The Dow is quite a silly index, for lack of a better word, and there's very little reason to use it. Mostly it's an index that talk show hosts on business television shows mention, since they feel that the public are more familiar with its name.

The Dow Jones consists of only 30 stocks. That in itself is a severe limitation of the index. The 30 largest stocks are not representative for the thousands of stocks on the US exchanges. It's an extremely narrow index.

The larger problem is in how the Dow Jones is calculated. It is a price weighted index. This means that you just add up all the share prices of the 30 constituent stocks and divide by 30. To be precise, you also need to divide by the index divisor, but that's just a technicality to arrive at consistent numbers.

If you stop and think about this for a moment, it should be very clear just how nuts this methodology really is. A stock with a higher share price will have a greater impact on the index. This is rooted in the very old way of thinking, that the stock price itself has some sort of analytical implication. That a share price of 100 makes a company more important than a share price of 10.

Keep in mind that we're not talking about market capitalization. Share price is not in any way related to how valuable a company is. A company with a share price of 10 could have 100,000,000 shares outstanding, while a company with a share price of 100 could have 10,000 shares outstanding. The share price by itself means absolutely nothing.

The Dow Jones Index and its methodology is a legacy product. There are plenty of better alternatives to use. On the professional side, the MSCI set of indexes are very popular. The core value of this set is that you'll get a consistent methodology on a global basis, covering anything you could possibly want. There are hundreds of MSCI indexes, classified by geography, style and sectors. For asset managers, this is the go-to set of indexes, but the drawback is that it's quite expensive to buy index constituents information. The value of buying access to a premium set of indexes for retail traders is also questionable. It would make more sense for most to look for broad indexes where the constituent information is available free of charge. For the US markets, the Standard & Poor indexes make for a good choice.

The most well-known of these indexes is of course the S&P 500 index, consisting of the largest 500 stocks on the US exchanges. Also of interest may be the S&P 400 mid cap index and the S&P 600 small cap index. Together these three indexes also form the S&P 1500 index.

Exactly which index you end up using doesn't matter as much as your reasons for it. Don't pick an index on random. Figure out what you're looking for, and pick an index to match.

In this book, the S&P 500 will be used most of the time. The ideas presented work fine with any broad enough index though. Your mileage may vary with more narrow indexes of course.

Market Capitalization

Market capitalization refers to how much a company is worth. Yes, it may very well be a needlessly complex sounding term for something very simple.

To understand what market capitalization, usually just called market cap, really is, just look at how it's calculated. Start by checking the total shares outstanding. That's the number of shares issued by a company, all in all. That means all shares outstanding, whether free floating or not. Next you simply multiply the number of shares with the current stock price. The number you get is the theoretical value of the company as a whole. It's theoretical, because if you were looking to buy the entire company the price would be quite different, as you see in any merger or corporate takeover bid.

Grouping stocks based on market cap often makes sense. Most market indexes have strict rules regarding market cap and focus one on one range. The S&P 500 Index is a large-cap index, which according to their standard means that any company needs to have a minimum market cap of $5.3 billion. That doesn't mean that any company larger than this is included, only that a company needs to fulfill this minimum market cap in order to be considered in the first place.

The lesser known S&P 400 Index is the mid-cap equivalent. To be a candidate for this index, a company needs to have a market cap between $750 million and $3.3 billion. The small-cap index S&P 600 covers stocks with a value between $400 million to $1.8 billion.

All of these indexes are weighted based on market cap. The higher value a company has the larger weight it will get in the index. Whether or not that makes sense depends very much on your point of view. It probably makes a lot of sense if the purpose of the index is to gauge the overall market health and long term development. It probably makes less sense if you aim to invest according to those principles.

Generally speaking, large caps tend to have lower volatility than small caps. They also tend to have less potential than small caps. It certainly doesn't mean that it's a bad idea to trade large caps. It's just a difference that you should be aware of.

Look at it this way. Apple started out as a small-cap company, like everyone else. Well, technically a nano-cap company or whatever term you prefer for a company run by two bearded hippies in a garage. It went through all the cycles of going from a small-cap to a mid-cap to a large-cap stock. I don't even want to calculate how many times that stock has doubled in value since 1976. Now the company is worth around $500 billion. That's half a trillion dollars. Around $100 billion more than the second largest company in the world. How likely is it to double again?

It's not impossible by any means. It's just a whole lot more difficult to double the stock price when you're trading at half a trillion dollars than it is when you're trading at half a million.

The risks tend to be higher with smaller companies, but so are the potential rewards.

Sectors

Classifying stocks by sectors is just a way to keep track of what the companies actually do. It's a good idea to be aware of sectors even if you don't apply any fundamental analysis. There's usually some sectors doing very well and others doing poorly. This can of course be identified using quantitative methods if you so prefer. Being aware of what's driving the market is important. If you're not looking at the sectors at all, you may be building up an overly large exposure towards a single sector or theme without even knowing it. Taking risk is necessary, but it should be done deliberately.

As of writing this text in early 2015, the energy sector has been taking a shelling for over half a year. Outperforming the S&P 500 during this period could easily have been done simply by not buying any energy stocks.

There are several schemes to classify stocks and the terminology may vary slightly. In the end, they are quite similar though and it doesn't matter much which scheme you settle on. I tend to use the GICS scheme, since it's a coherent global standard and easily available in most market data platforms. It also has the advantage of being four levels deep, which can be of value at times.

On the top level, the GICS scheme has ten sectors, which I'll be using to describe stocks in this book. These sectors are consumer discretionary, consumer staples, energy, financials, industrials, information technology, materials, telecommunication services, utilities and health care. If you'd like to dig deeper, each sector is divided into industry groups, industries and sub-industries. For most of us, the sector level is quite sufficient.

4
Does Trend Following Work on Stocks?

The concept of trend following was originally developed for futures trading. This is a world apart from the equity markets. Frankly, traditional trend following simply does not work for equities.

Trend following is conceptually very simple. When prices start moving in one direction, whether up or down, you jump on the bandwagon. If prices start moving up, go long. If they start moving down, go short. Then you hold that position as long as it continues. Usually this is done by having a trailing stop behind the price. This means that you only exit after losing a certain amount on the trade from the best reading. You'll never buy at the bottom and you'll never sell at the top, but you'll always participate in the middle.

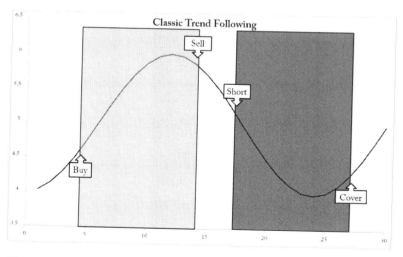

Figure 4-1 Basic Trend Following

As far as trading strategies goes, trend following is quite dumb. I don't mean that it's dumb to trade it, just that it's based on very little information. Compared to complex strategies, taking a large number of factors into account, it's a dumb strategy. This dumb strategy has however shown very strong results for the past thirty odd years, and according to some research it's even performed remarkably well for hundreds of years (Kaminski & Greyserman, 2014). There have been ups and downs and at times there have even been multiple years in a row where the trend following industry lost money. But in the end, the overall return for the past few decades is very strong.

The trend following hedge fund business has grown fast and is now worth in excess of $300 billion. Many of these fund managers have been around for decades and show some of the best compound return figures in the industry. Quest Partners, Fort Investment Management, Chesapeake, Campbell, ISAM, Mulvaney, Transtrend and Winton, to name just a few.

It's very difficult for anyone to argue that systematic trend following on futures doesn't work. The empirical evidence is simply too overwhelming.

Classic trend following is done on futures. The normal way to execute this strategy is to follow trends on a large set of futures markets, covering all major asset classes. Professional trend followers trade commodities, interest rates, currencies and of course equity indexes. The reason for this approach is very simple. If you apply a trend following model to a single market, you're just gambling. Even if you apply it to many markets in a single asset class, the success probabilities are low.

Any given market or even asset class can, and often will, have extended periods of time where trend following doesn't work. When the markets are moving sideways or quickly changing directions then trend followers lose money. For any individual market or sector, this can keep happening for years. In extreme cases, even a decade. The core premise of trend following is therefore based on diversification. By trading all of these different asset classes at the same time, the probabilities are very high that something makes enough money to compensate for the losses in other asset classes.

If the assets you trade have low correlation to each other, you'll be able to grind out more return at lower risk. It's all about taking the portfolio perspective instead of the position perspective. This way of thinking is a key point that separates professionals from hobby traders. Only the portfolio level matters. When trading multiple assets with low or negative correlation, you can achieve higher return at lower risk. If the timing of the gains and losses of different assets is very different, you'll be able to raise your overall trading level for higher returns at the same risk, or maintain your returns at overall lower risk.

The big money in trend following is made on the extreme trends. A small number of trends that keep on going for month after month, and sometimes year after year, will generate outsized returns. Since you just keep the successful trades, you'll stay in these trades. The failed trades will take a small loss and exit fast. So you can afford to have many losses, as long as you get these big winners from time to time.

In the end, trend following boils down to statistics. It's about making sure that you'll have favorable probabilities of gains in the long run at acceptable volatility.

The most important thing to understand about trend following is just how reliant it is on diversification. It cannot be stressed enough that for trend following to work reliably, you need a diverse set of markets to trade. If you trade too few markets or too similar markets, you are relying on luck. You might have great results or you might have horrible results, but it will be luck dependent. Pick the right set of markets in the right year, and you'll do fine. But for those of us not content at leaving our fate to luck, a broad set of markets is needed to have sufficient statistical basis for a trend following approach.

If you apply a standard trend following model to stocks, you will most likely lose money. These models weren't developed for use on single stocks and they will not perform on them. There are several reasons why it's a bad idea to take an approach meant for diversified futures and applying it on stocks.

Both stocks and futures have a price series that can be analyzed. It may appear as if the difference really shouldn't be that big. After all, it's just another time series to trade. Well, there are a couple of significant differences still. The first one is of practical nature.

Futures trading allows for very high leverage. Even more than that. It allows you to completely disregard leverage. It's not a limiting factor. Being able to take on large notional exposure is an important part of traditional trend following. When trading futures, the normal way of deciding position size is to simply look at the risk side. You look at the volatility of the instrument, correlations to current positions and such factors. Cash availability just isn't a factor. Futures traders always have a large amount of available cash. Most professional traders only use 10-20 percent of the cash as margin. The rest can then be placed in money markets or fixed income instruments, both for safe keeping and to generate interest income. This has a few advantages. First, you can get a relatively risk free return on your excess capital. This may not be so important at the moment, when yields are at all-time lows. Right now, you may not get much return on that capital, but in the past you could get a substantial boost to your bottom line simply by putting excess capital into short term money market and treasury instruments.

Second, you can focus on targeting a specific risk level without regard to what cash is available. You can afford to take on large positions in slow moving markets, such as money market and fixed income. In short, leverage is absolutely irrelevant when you're trading futures.

It must be said of course, that you shouldn't be confusing leverage with risk. They are utterly different things and high leverage doesn't necessarily mean high risk, any more than low exposure needs to mean low risk. Risk is never irrelevant. Leverage however, is in itself not a very useful measurement.

That is, unless you're trading cash instruments, like stocks. With stocks, you need to pay for your purchases upfront, more or less. You may be able to get a bit of leverage by borrowing against your other stocks, but it's very limited. When you're dealing with cash instruments, you've always got to deal with the possibility of running out of cash. It's an added complication and a limitation. It is however not the most important difference between stocks and futures.

The real killer is correlations. Stocks are very homogenous as a group. They have a very high internal correlation. That, in plain English, means that stocks tend to behave more or less the same. Naturally there are individual differences between stocks, but the fact of the matter is that in a bull market almost all of them will go up. In a bear market, almost all of them will go down. Diversification doesn't help you very much.

Whether you hold ten stocks or fifty, you're still mostly long beta. It's ok to be long beta, as long as you do it deliberately. There's money to be made being long beta in the right times, and that's all dandy. The problem comes if you're unaware that you're making money on beta. In every bull market, the stock pickers come out of the woodworks. The war stories about making money on buying the right stocks are told over and over again in the media and in the blogs. Come bear market, the same people are conspicuously missing.

There is some diversification to be had in stocks, but not that much. You should always diversify. In stocks however, the diversification effect will be saturated much faster. Holding twenty stocks is better than holding five, but there's not much to be gained by holding fifty stocks.

Given the high correlations and the overwhelming beta component to stocks, it's unrealistic to expect that your returns will not be highly dependent on the index. Don't expect to achieve the same yearly returns regardless of whether the equity markets as a whole are moving up or down. If you deal in stocks, you will be highly dependent on the overall market environment.

Then there's the matter of the short side. Even when dealing with multiple asset classes, the short side is very difficult. Professional futures trend followers make very little money on the short side over time. Some years it helps, but most years it doesn't. The short side is very tricky for a variety of reasons. It's not just a matter of turning the chart upside down. That's an illusion. Two things are very different with short trades.

The first one may be a little surprising. It has to do with the longer time periods that these types of strategies employ. If you buy an asset and it goes in your favor, it will grow larger with success. Your exposure will grow larger as the gains grow. If the position should move up by one percent per day, that one percent will mean increasingly larger profits in dollar as the position grows.

On the short side, you'll find the opposite. Your position will shrink for every day it moves in your favor. If your short position declines in price by one percent per day, that percent will now mean less and less to you, since your exposure is going down too. Over the long run, this effect has a detrimental impact on short positions.

The other reason for short positions being troublesome is more straight forward. They're just not as well behaved. Stocks are prone to rapid volatility expansions in bear markets. They are not as orderly as when the sailing is clear. There may be surprises now and then in a bull market too, but in a bear market it's only surprises. That stock that was moving in such a nice bear market channel for the past three months can suddenly jump up and wipe out all your gains in a day. Those risk measurements you just calculated for your position sizing could go right out the window at any moment.

Then of course you have the added borrowing costs and the often limited availability of stocks that could be borrowed for short sale.

Holding stocks during a bear market, whether long or short, is like watching popcorn in the microwave oven. No matter how much you stare at them and try to will them to stay calm, it's just a matter of time before another random piece of corn blows up right in-front of your eyes.

Trading the short side is difficult in all asset classes, but most of all in stocks. While for example commodities can at times have a strong negative bias, fueled by the cost of carry, there's no such advantage in stocks. Storage cost and other factors can make some commodity futures move down for years in a seemingly smooth line. Not so with stocks. When stocks are in a bear market, they behave very differently than in bull market. Measured over longer periods, very few people make money from shorting.

Then of course, there's a matter of what stocks to apply your trend following model to. With futures, you can include everything. Throwing in a hundred or more futures markets into your strategy isn't a problem. But with stocks? Do you pick a few stocks manually to trade? A whole index? Do you trade all the stocks in the index? At what exposure?

No, stocks are simply different. They require special care. And it's a very bad idea to trade simple trend models on them.

Trend following doesn't work on stocks. But momentum models do.

The Problem with Trend Following on Stocks

When you make claims such as that trend following doesn't work on stocks, it's usually a good idea to duck and cover, not to get hit by the incoming egg and rotten tomatoes. A few readers probably already put down the book to stock up on suitable blunt objects to throw in my general direction. Perhaps some actual demonstrations could help. Let's look at some trend following trading models and see how they perform on stocks.

The trading models shown in this section are reasonably valid in terms of concept. The investment universe is the S&P 500 stocks at any given day. That means that the historical index membership is considered and a stock is only allowed to be bought if it's a part of the index on the day in question. If a stock leaves the index, it's sold right away.

All historical members of this index are considered, and that includes delisted issues. Even if a stock has gone bankrupt years ago, that stock must still be taken into consideration in a proper simulation. For a simulation to be valid, it has to replicate reality as close as possible. The simulation shouldn't be aware of the future any more than the rest of us.

In the same manner, mergers, splits and similar corporate actions are taken into account. Dividends are of course accounted for, as this is a major source of error if ignored. The simulations are carefully constructed to replicate reality as close as possible.

Standard Trend Following Model on Stocks

Let's start with a classic. This trading model is a simple, symmetrical trend following approach meant for futures trading. It's a medium term model and when run on a broad set of futures markets, it has shown to closely replicate the very strong returns that the CTA industry has a whole has achieved for the past 30 to 40 years.

This is also, incidentally, the same trend following model that I used in my first book (Clenow, 2013). The trading rules are very simple. I'll give you the concept first and the details after.

This trading model can go long and short. It goes long in a positive trend and only short in a negative trend. If a stock is in a positive trend and makes a new 50 day high, we buy it. If it's in a negative trend and makes a 50 day low, we short it. A trailing stop loss will be used, equivalent of three days' worth of normal trading range. Position sizes will be calculated to achieve approximately the same risk in each position, using a simple formula based on ATR which will be explain in detail in chapter 8.

The rules:

- A dual 50 and 100 moving average used for trend filter. If the 50 day moving average is above the 100 day, the stock is considered to be in a positive trend, else negative.
- 50 day breakout in the direction of the trend triggers trade entry.
- Risk parity position sizing.
- A trailing stop of 3 times current ATR is set in place.
- Only stocks that were part of the S&P 500 Index on a given day were allowed to be traded on that day. Historical index constituents and delisted stocks accounted for.
- All corporate actions, including cash dividends are properly accounted for.

This simple model shows very strong results, if applied to a broad set of cross asset futures. This is the game played by the CTA industry. This strategy was originally used by a couple of traders in Chicago that no one really took seriously, until they started making very large amounts of money. What was once a fringe trading method is now a 300 billion dollar global industry. We know from empirical evidence that models like this one work well. At least on futures.

As a quick demonstration, let's start by seeing with a simple model like this can do when applied to a broad set of futures markets. After all, since I'm claiming that the rules above work well on that asset class, it's only fair that I demonstrate it. Figure 4-2 shows the result of applying this straight forward trend following model to a set of 70 futures markets, covering all asset classes. Despite having had a couple of bad years recently, the overall returns are very strong. The compound annual return was about 17% and the maximum drawdown was around 27%.

This demonstrates that the principle as such is valid. Trend following works, at least on futures.

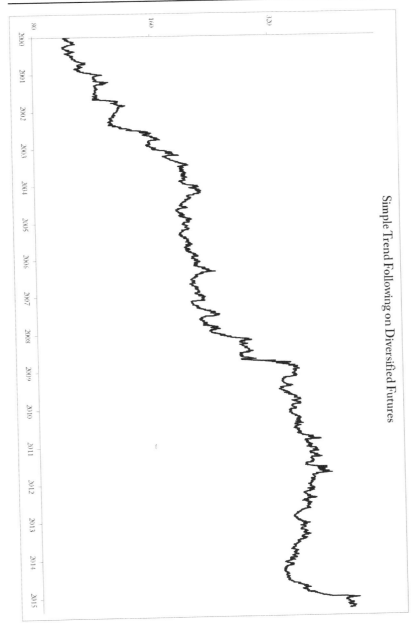

Figure 4-2 Simple Trend Following on Futures

Table 4-1 Simple Trend Following on Futures

	Jan (%)	Feb (%)	Mar (%)	Apr (%)	May (%)	Jun (%)	Jul (%)	Aug (%)	Sep (%)	Oct (%)	Nov (%)	Dec (%)	Year (%)
2000	3.0	0.1	1.1	-4.3	0.8	2.6	3.3	1.0	5.2	-2.1	0.2	1.9	**13.3**
2001	14.3	-3.2	3.8	7.8	-7.2	1.3	1.3	3.0	-2.0	17.9	4.7	-3.0	**42.4**
2002	-2.9	-2.7	-0.8	2.6	-0.5	5.2	9.1	-4.8	4.3	5.7	-6.5	0.3	**8.0**
2003	-0.3	9.1	5.2	-7.0	5.1	5.0	-3.5	2.6	5.2	0.3	6.2	-4.0	**24.8**
2004	4.7	1.9	9.2	-1.6	-6.1	-0.7	-4.1	1.7	-2.5	0.6	0.9	7.7	**11.0**
2005	-0.6	0.2	0.3	-2.1	-1.8	5.5	0.4	1.3	-0.4	-0.2	-0.9	3.6	**5.2**
2006	-3.6	5.5	-4.3	9.7	3.7	-3.4	-3.0	-4.3	3.6	-0.3	3.6	5.4	**11.8**
2007	0.5	-0.1	-7.1	-0.2	3.8	8.3	3.4	-4.3	3.5	2.0	5.3	0.4	**15.6**
2008	3.9	6.8	24.4	-9.5	0.0	4.2	4.7	-9.1	2.1	7.2	26.7	11.5	**91.6**
2009	0.7	-1.2	1.9	-9.5	-0.2	7.8	-7.2	1.0	0.8	3.7	-2.2	7.6	**1.8**
2010	-4.2	-4.2	2.6	3.5	0.7	-0.8	2.8	3.4	0.8	2.1	10.8	-3.7	**13.8**
2011	7.1	4.0	-1.4	-1.6	5.2	-5.1	-6.0	3.9	4.0	10.5	-12.5	-0.2	**5.8**
2012	-1.3	-0.4	3.2	-0.9	-2.3	9.4	-9.0	5.7	-1.3	-3.8	-3.3	-2.3	**-7.3**
2013	2.9	6.0	-3.6	-0.5	2.2	-2.9	0.2	-1.2	-4.9	-1.3	1.5	1.5	**-0.8**
2014	-5.7	-1.3	4.6	-2.8	0.8	3.9	3.3	1.7	4.2	10.4	-2.4	4.9	**22.4**

With stocks however, not so much. Figure 4-3 shows the return over time that this standard trend model would have generated. Over the period from 2000 to end of 2014, you would have ended up with a loss of almost 30%. Actually, you would have lost a lot more than that. The simulation here doesn't even take commissions into account. This would have been a disaster strategy.

The settings used for this simulation is not the cause. If you change the trend filter, the breakout period or the stop loss, it will still look disastrous. This isn't a matter of some details or something that could be optimized away. You can try hundreds of iterations and your results will be very similar. What we're seeing is a problem with the core concept.

Figure 4-4 and Figure 4-5 show typical trade charts for this model, applied to stocks. These figures show both some good trades and some really frustrating ones.

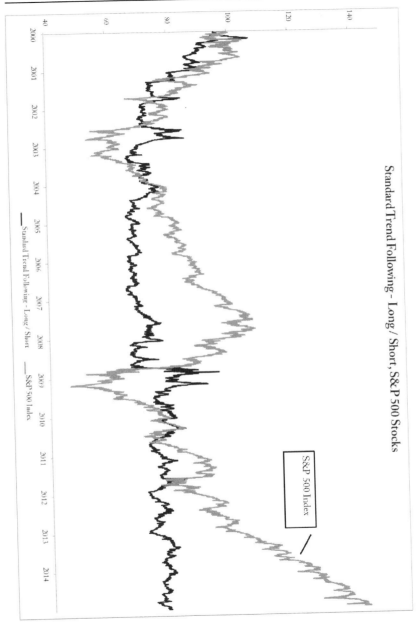

Figure 4-3 Standard Long/Short Trend Following on Stocks

Table 4-2 Long Short Trend Following on Stocks

	Jan (%)	Feb (%)	Mar (%)	Apr (%)	May (%)	Jun (%)	Jul (%)	Aug (%)	Sep (%)	Oct (%)	Nov (%)	Dec (%)	Year (%)
2000	3.0	-4.6	8.8	-7.6	-5.0	1.6	-2.4	-2.2	-2.1	3.4	-3.4	3.3	-7.9
2001	-0.6	-7.9	-0.6	-0.5	-7.9	-0.4	0.1	1.6	1.3	8.1	-10.5	-3.6	-20.3
2002	1.3	0.0	1.5	-3.2	1.9	0.0	5.6	5.6	-2.8	1.5	-5.8	-4.2	0.7
2003	-3.0	-2.7	1.4	-2.6	0.0	6.5	0.5	0.1	3.9	-6.0	4.2	0.5	2.3
2004	1.4	0.2	2.6	-4.3	-2.4	-5.4	1.2	0.2	-0.6	-0.8	-2.3	4.4	-6.0
2005	0.7	-2.2	0.4	0.0	1.0	-3.3	1.8	2.4	0.0	2.1	-4.4	-1.0	-2.8
2006	-0.2	3.0	-1.9	-0.2	0.7	-1.3	1.0	2.3	-4.3	-1.0	1.2	2.6	1.6
2007	1.0	1.0	-1.3	1.0	0.8	3.6	1.4	2.2	-4.4	2.0	-1.1	-0.7	5.4
2008	2.2	-8.0	1.4	-0.9	-1.4	0.5	6.1	-3.2	-3.3	5.9	12.5	11.4	23.3
2009	-10.8	3.0	9.4	-9.7	-3.2	0.5	-3.7	-0.7	-0.8	3.0	-0.2	4.0	-10.5
2010	1.0	-3.5	0.3	2.6	4.2	-3.4	-1.9	-6.3	-0.8	-1.2	1.2	2.2	-5.7
2011	2.0	2.4	-0.2	-1.9	1.2	-0.3	-2.8	1.2	2.3	4.2	-8.0	-3.5	-3.9
2012	-0.4	1.7	3.1	3.4	-1.5	3.6	-4.9	-1.4	-0.4	0.6	0.1	-3.1	0.5
2013	1.5	4.1	0.8	2.3	0.3	0.5	-2.4	2.1	-2.9	-0.6	1.1	0.9	7.8
2014	1.3	0.3	-2.8	-0.1	-1.5	1.2	2.1	-4.0	1.5	-0.6	-1.6	2.7	-1.5

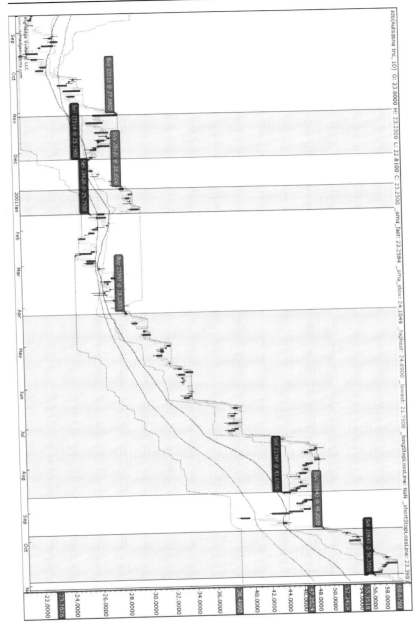

Figure 4-4 Trend Following Trade Chart, Autozone

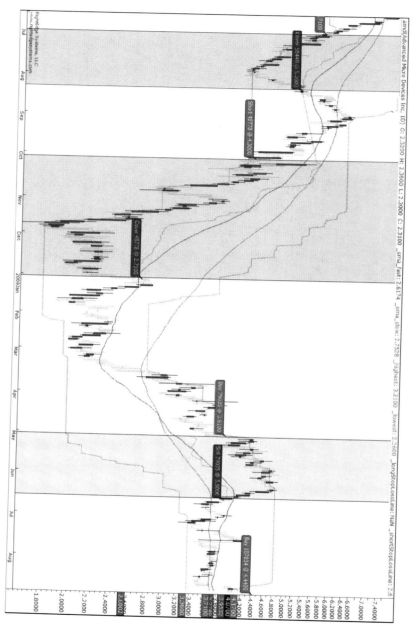

Figure 4-5 Trend Following Trade Chart, AMD

On those trade charts, it may look as if the stop is a bit too close. Perhaps they are, but it really doesn't matter much. Double the stop distances and you get almost the same portfolio results. The winners will stay in longer and gain more, but the losers will at the same time cost you more too.

Do you want to stop and guess what the biggest problem is? The model above has several problems, but there's one that is of enormously more importance than the rest.

Yes, it's the short side. The short side of regular trend following, as applied on cross asset futures, is a concern. Even seasoned professional trend followers tend to make little to no money on the short side of trend following. When you're dealing with diversified futures, covering everything from currencies, rates, commodities and all other major asset classes, then the short side does have a clear benefit. Its main purpose is to improve the return skew of the strategy in the long run. Not to make money in its own right. If you're only dealing in equities, don't bother going too deep into these things though. It doesn't work the same way for stocks anyhow.

What you need to understand is simply that using a trend following approach to short stocks is a very bad idea. You're not going to make any money doing it. Trend following simply doesn't work for shorting stocks. Just. Say. No.

Can we forget about the short side and move on? Good. For the rest of the book, there will be no more shorting.

Let's do another run for the same trading model as above, with only one change. This time we only trade the long side. Figure 4-6 shows the result of this simulation. Now it starts looking a little more interesting, doesn't it? Not only do we get a positive return, we actually get more money in the end than the index.

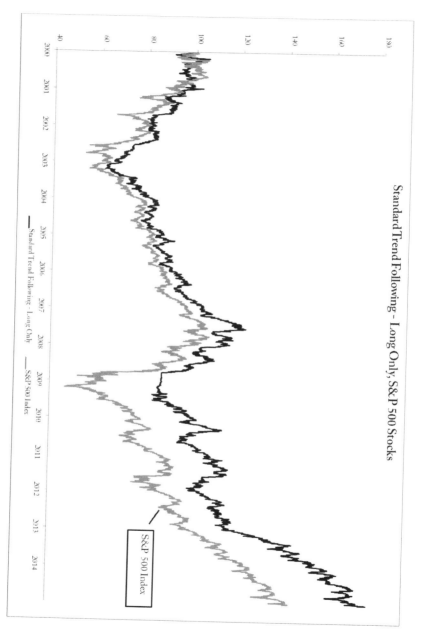

Figure 4-6 Standard Trend Following, Long Only

Table 4-3 Long Only Trend Following on Stocks

	Jan (%)	Feb (%)	Mar (%)	Apr (%)	May (%)	Jun (%)	Jul (%)	Aug (%)	Sep (%)	Oct (%)	Nov (%)	Dec (%)	Year (%)
2000	3.0	-8.3	9.1	1.3	-4.8	3.0	-3.9	-1.8	3.6	2.4	-2.4	1.2	**1.1**
2001	1.3	-4.5	-2.7	-3.7	1.9	1.1	-0.2	-0.6	-1.8	-7.5	-2.7	0.3	**-18.0**
2002	1.2	0.4	1.4	-0.1	0.5	-3.3	-4.0	-5.3	-1.6	-1.6	-0.7	-2.2	**-14.3**
2003	-2.0	-5.6	-1.0	2.3	2.7	8.3	1.1	0.5	5.7	-3.4	6.3	1.5	**16.6**
2004	1.1	2.0	2.4	-2.4	-1.1	-1.4	1.6	-1.2	-1.2	2.5	0.2	5.0	**7.3**
2005	-0.3	0.8	2.5	-3.2	-2.0	2.3	0.7	3.7	-1.3	2.7	-4.7	4.7	**5.6**
2006	-0.3	3.8	0.8	1.3	-0.1	-1.2	-0.4	0.9	2.0	0.0	2.6	2.8	**12.9**
2007	1.1	2.0	-1.0	4.2	4.3	5.3	-0.4	-3.6	-4.6	4.7	-0.1	-1.5	**10.4**
2008	-0.3	-7.9	0.1	-1.2	2.5	2.0	-3.3	-6.2	0.9	-7.1	-4.7	0.0	**-22.9**
2009	0.2	-0.6	-1.7	1.3	1.2	2.2	-2.7	4.4	-0.7	3.4	0.1	6.1	**13.5**
2010	1.8	-2.6	3.6	5.4	4.7	-11.4	-3.7	2.2	-0.6	4.0	1.5	1.7	**5.6**
2011	3.5	0.6	0.5	1.8	2.9	-0.4	1.1	-4.0	-4.4	-3.7	0.3	-0.4	**-2.4**
2012	1.3	2.5	3.0	4.5	1.0	-6.3	4.6	-0.5	0.2	2.5	1.2	-1.6	**12.7**
2013	3.4	4.8	2.0	4.6	2.3	3.7	-1.9	6.7	-4.4	4.0	3.5	0.9	**33.0**
2014	2.6	-3.2	6.1	-0.7	0.2	1.8	3.4	-2.1	2.3	-2.4	1.6	1.7	**11.4**

Actually we don't get more money than the index. I was just teasing you a bit, and trying to make a point. There are two problems with the comparison in Figure 4-6. First, there are no costs taken into account. Over 14 years, the commission costs will add up and that'll push your line down a bit. But that's not the main problem with the comparison.

The stocks are all adjusted for dividends, but the standard S&P 500 price index is not. The simulation handled all the actual dividends that came in, and therefore profited from them. The index on the other hand simply disregards these dividends as if they never happened. If you have dividends on one side, we have to have it on the other. Comparing with a price index is therefore highly misleading. We need to compare with a total return index.

Total return means that all actual sources of return are taken into account. When a stock goes ex-div, it usually drops in price by about the same amount as the dividend to be paid. As this happens, standard price indexes are negatively affected, even though no values really changed from an investor's point of view. The share price dropped, but you got the equivalent cash. A total return index adjusts properly for this.

That means that a total return index will show higher return than a price index. During shorter time periods the difference may not be that large, but once you're dealing with multiple years or decades, the difference will become quite substantial. Note that whenever you hear about the S&P 500 index in the media, they always refer to the price index. If it's just about the day's move, then it really doesn't matter. If they make some statement about how the S&P moved a certain percent in a decade, then it's misleading at best.

Let's do that last comparison again, but this time with the S&P 500 Total Return Index. This is after all the most proper way to compare our performance. The resulting Figure 4-7 is less flattering. Over 14 years, we managed to come out with a clear underperformance against the index. Sure, we did manage to keep the maximum drawdown a little more reasonable, mostly because the long only trend model stopped buying when every single stock was crashing back in 2008. This however is not a viable strategy. If you want a return curve like this, just go buy a passive index tracking ETF.

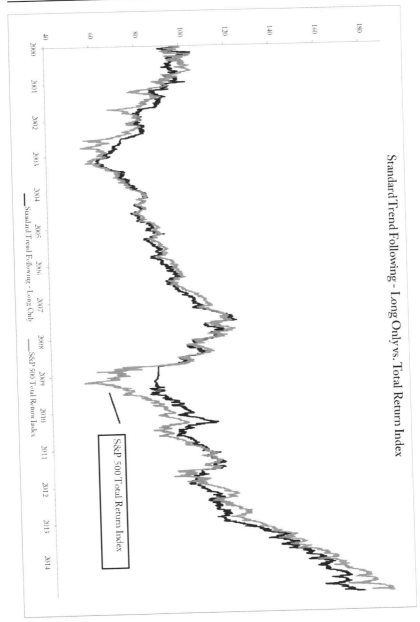

Figure 4-7 Stocks trend following compared with total return index

Someone's surely pointing out that trend following on stocks did produce profits. That's clear from the graphs above, at least if you ditch the short side. That's absolutely true. The problem is that it doesn't add any value. It creates a lot of work and potential risks, but it doesn't yield any benefits. Compared with a simple passive holding of the index tracker, applying classic trend following on stocks does not appear to be a very attractive alternative.

All Time High Model

Let's try another approach then. One method proposed by Cole Wilcox and Eric Crittenden at Longboard Asset Management (Wilcox & Crittenden, 2005) is to use all time high as the entry criteria. In their study from 2005, they use a very large stock universe, buy on all time high and sell at a trailing stop set at a distance of ten times the 40 day average true range. I've attempted to replicate it as close as possible based on the details in their document, but with one main difference. I've used only stocks part of the S&P 500 Index, to have a valid benchmark.

In their research paper, they say that they take all signals which implies that they scale all open positions to accommodate for incoming and outgoing stocks. This would mean that you could potentially own hundreds of stocks simultaneously and doesn't appear to be a realistic approach for most investors. I'll use a more realistic method of risk parity sizing, targeting a daily average impact of 10 basis points per stock. This is a very simple but effective method and will be explained in more detail in chapter 8. For now, I'll also leave out the position rebalancing that they're using. I'll explain in later chapters why rebalancing is a good idea and how it can further improve results.

This is a simplified version of their model but based on the same core logic.

Trading Rules:

- Buy on all-time high, if cash is available.
- No leverage employed.
- Positions sized using simple risk parity, targeting an equal initial risk allocated to each stock.

- No rebalancing.
- Trailing stop loss at 10 times the initial ATR, using a 50 day calculation period.

This trading model shows pretty decent results. It's still not a recommended approach and it still has lots of kinks to work out, but it's better than applying a classic futures model. From the simulation results in Figure 4-8 it's clear that the momentum approach used here has a value. Buying the all-time high breakouts did pay off. It's also clear that this model isn't ready for show time. To be perfectly fair though, it's a demo built to demonstrate a concept. As such, it's both valid and good research.

As could be expected, this model suffers losses during bear markets, such as 2000 to 2003. During such phases, this model performs more or less on par with the overall equity markets. In bull market phases, it tends to outperform, even though we saw a much larger outperformance during the 2003 to 2007 bull market than we've seen in the rally starting in 2009.

The flattening profile in 2008 to 2009 isn't a concern and actually makes perfect sense. It would take some time before stocks start seeing all-time high values again after the 2008 disaster, and therefore would take time before exposure is built up again.

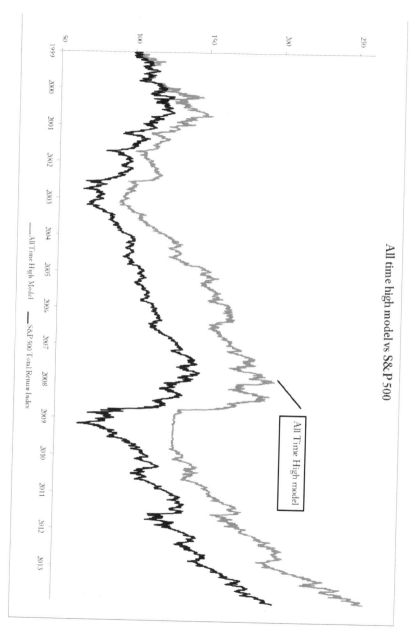

Figure 4-8 All-time high model

Figure 4-9 shows an example of one of many trades for this trading model. The thick line indicates the all-time high level, while the dotted line shows the stop loss point. In this Apple trade chart, you can see how the stock was bought when it first hit its all-time high value and a stop was put in place. The stock needs to close below the stop in order to exit the position on the following day.

Table 4-4 All Time High Model

	Jan (%)	Feb (%)	Mar (%)	Apr (%)	May (%)	Jun (%)	Jul (%)	Aug (%)	Sep (%)	Oct (%)	Nov (%)	Dec (%)	Year (%)
2000	3.0	-3.7	13.8	-1.8	-2.6	0.3	1.1	0.5	9.2	0.2	-5.4	-7.3	5.5
2001	4.6	-4.9	-3.0	-5.6	4.3	1.7	-1.6	-0.4	-2.3	-4.4	0.0	1.6	-10.1
2002	4.1	0.8	1.1	1.1	2.8	-1.6	-2.7	-11.5	-1.1	0.4	-0.8	-4.2	-11.8
2003	0.9	-3.2	0.2	4.2	1.8	5.1	1.3	1.1	4.1	0.9	5.1	2.4	26.4
2004	2.5	2.3	3.9	1.6	-1.1	-0.9	1.6	-2.1	-0.9	5.3	1.0	6.5	21.4
2005	2.3	2.7	5.2	-1.5	-2.2	1.9	0.5	3.2	-0.7	4.1	-1.6	6.0	21.4
2006	0.5	2.1	-0.6	0.4	-1.8	-1.0	-2.4	-1.2	2.8	-0.1	3.2	2.0	3.8
2007	0.8	2.6	-2.3	4.0	2.9	4.4	-2.2	-3.9	0.4	6.5	-3.1	1.5	11.6
2008	-0.5	-5.2	1.4	1.7	2.3	3.9	-0.9	-10.0	-0.5	-8.4	-13.6	-1.8	-28.7
2009	-0.8	0.3	-1.1	0.6	-0.1	-0.1	0.0	0.1	-0.4	0.1	-0.3	4.1	2.1
2010	1.5	-2.5	3.9	2.9	1.7	-2.9	-1.1	1.9	0.0	4.4	3.7	2.1	16.5
2011	1.1	-0.4	1.5	3.3	3.6	0.6	2.1	-3.4	-2.6	-2.7	4.5	3.2	11.0
2012	0.6	0.4	3.3	2.0	3.3	-3.9	4.4	1.7	-1.3	1.9	-1.5	-1.4	9.4
2013	1.5	3.1	2.3	4.7	2.1	-0.2	-0.4	7.4	-3.8	4.2	1.5	1.8	26.6
2014	1.6	-2.8	3.0	-1.0	-1.3	3.6	2.9	-2.5	4.7	-1.7	4.2	1.6	12.7

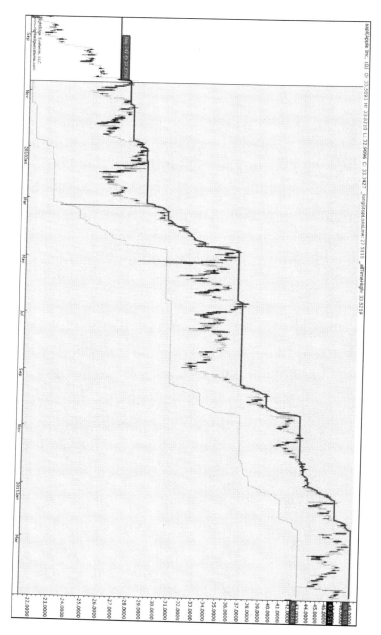

Figure 4-9 All-time high model - Apple trade

There are a couple of problems with this all-time high approach. The first concern is that the stock selection is quite random. Whatever stock makes an all-time high first will be bought, until we run out of cash. The fact that a stock made its high first doesn't necessarily mean that it's a better candidate than others. The second problem is that a stock will be held until it hits its stop. That means that a stock could in theory move sideways for years without being kicked out.

That stock would end up taking up valuable cash in the portfolio without showing any performance for it. Even if the stock moves up, it could be moving up very slowly while other stocks are moving up fast. We would end up holding poorly performing stocks for much longer than what would make sense.

However, this model does show us that there might be something to the general concept. The methodology needs more work, but there's something there. What this model indicates is that during normal to strong markets, momentum stocks seem to outperform. Let's see if we can't make something more solid out of that.

Trend Following on Single Stocks

Trend following on single stocks is a bad idea. Your success will be completely luck dependent.

Single stock trend following would mean that you pick a stock, or perhaps a few of them, and apply a trend model just to them. Proponents of this approach usually point out how well it would have worked on Apple, Google, Microsoft etc. Those stocks are usually picked as examples, just because they had great performance in the past. They are famous companies because they did well. The strategy of buying Microsoft 1985 and holding it for 15 years isn't trend following. That's just wishful thinking of buying the right stock at the right time.

Even for such great performers, most trend models didn't work that well. Sure, the stock price might have gained massively in a decade or two but usually there's heavy volatility along the way. You get pushed in and out of your positions often, reducing your profits. Yes, you could move the stop really, really far away. Of course, the further away you move it, the closer you get to a buy and hold strategy.

Let's take Apple as an example, since it's usually brought up in these discussions. We'll take a standard trend following model, based on buying positive breakouts in a bull market and shorting negative breakouts in a bear market. A trailing stop will be used, as is common with trend following models. Bear in mind that we're deliberately picking a stock which is known to have had an extreme price development in the past. If any stock works, it should be something like this one.

Applying a classic, medium term trend following model which has shown excellent results on futures for several decades on Apple turned out to be profitable. You'd end up with an annualized gain of nearly 10%. Not bad, huh? This model uses a stop distance of three times the average true range, which is a reasonable distance for a medium term model.

If we move the stop away to double that distance, this model did even better. Now we're seeing annualized gains of 15%! Clearly trend following worked.

No, not really.

The first problem here is that the initial version, while giving you 10% yearly return on average, saw a maximum loss of 48% and it took years to recover it. Not too attractive return for such risk, is it? The second and more profitable iteration with wider stops may have seen gains of 15%, but it also saw losses of 60%.

But then again, that's not the larger concern here. The big concern is that if you would simply stop mucking about with a trend following model and just buy and hold the stock, you would have gotten 26% annualized return. Figure 4-10 shows the performance of standard trend models on Apple, compared to simply buying and holding the stock.

If this is what trend following models do on extreme performers like Apple, you can imagine how poorly it looks for regular old stocks.

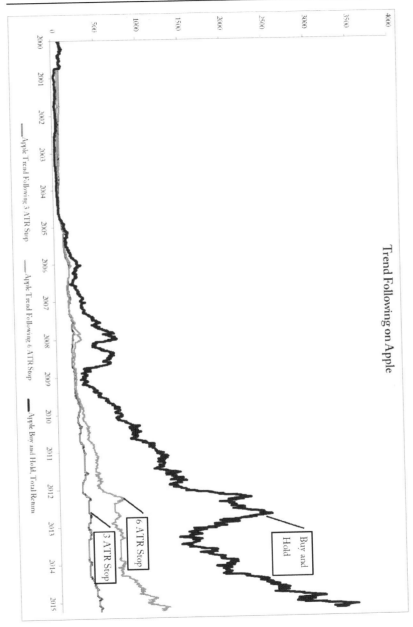

Figure 4-10 Trend Following on Apple

What I'm trying to say here is that trend following on a single, selected stock is an illusion. It's very easy to find a stock that did great in the past and conclude that you should have applied a trend following model to it, with extremely wide stops. Yes, perhaps so. And you should also have bought real estate in the 80s.

It boils down to the illusion of the so called Ten Bagger. The idea that trend following on stocks will help you ride that 1,000% stock. Well, no it won't. That's not trend following. That's selectively picking stocks that did extremely well in the past and dreaming of having bought them twenty years ago and never sold them.

The Semantics of Trend Following

You may be wondering if we're not just splitting hairs here. Equity momentum strategies versus trend following. Why use different terminology and why insist that trend following doesn't work on stocks?

The reason is that it really is a very different strategy. If you expand the scope of trend following to mean 'buy anything that makes money' then trend following is every single trading strategy you can think of. Trend following, as the term is used in the asset management business, has traditionally been developed for and used on the futures markets. It's about buying positive trend and shorting the negative trends, usually employing a trailing stop loss or exiting when the trend strength fails by other measurements. It requires a set of broad, diversified markets to function properly over time and it usually performs quite poorly on any single asset class alone.

Sometimes you'll see professional asset managers talk about trend following on stocks and even show you strong, real life performance. Usually, if you look closer, you'll see that what they're doing is a lot more like momentum strategies than trend following. Sometimes they might use the term trend following for marketing reasons. It's a better known term and it requires less explanations. There's nothing wrong with that, as long as their investors understand what they're buying. But if you want to learn how the sauce is made, how to construct your own strategies, then it's very important that you understand the differences between trend following and systematic equity momentum strategies.

5
The Momentum Effect

When a stock has been going up for a while, the likelihood of it continuing up is greater than for it to turn around. A stock which is moving up faster than other stocks is likely to continue to move up faster than other stocks. This, in essence, is the momentum effect.

What makes the momentum effect comfortable to rely on is not only that it has worked very well in the past, but also that it makes logical sense. It's a phenomenon in the market which is not likely to go away, because it's part of basic human nature. Everyone likes a winner.

According to some rather outdated academic theories, stock prices adjust instantly to all publicly known information and are therefore always priced at fair value. Anyone who's ever bought or sold a stock knows of course that this is not the case. Stocks move up and down all the time and it's very difficult to explain at the time why they are moving. It's usually easy to look back at a multi-year bull market, or bear market, and explain what happened and why. It's far more difficult while it's happening. Even today when financial information is readily available to anyone with a computer and an internet browser, facts are far from clear.

Just read the financial news during a busy day in the market for a demonstration. It can be quite comical at times really, especially when there's some more significant news coming out. At first, the market might be at -0.2% in the morning. News ticker updates with "Market down on FED fears". Two hours later, the market is at +0.2% and the news ticker proclaims "Market positive on FED hopes". The announcements finally come out, and the market dips down to -0.5%. News tells us that the market is falling on FED disappointment. As the market finally closes at +0.5% the news concludes that the market rallied on the positive FED announcement.

Following such news can be maddening. You need a sense of humor in this business. On the shorter time scale, like in the example above, the disconnect is obvious to most people. The market was really just flat and who knows what, if any effect that announcement really had. But even on a larger scale, over longer time periods, the same phenomenon is common. If you wait long enough to have the benefit of historical hindsight, you can probably find some real reasons for larger price moves. However, by then it's far too late. Finding reasons for price moves becomes an academic pursuit with very little practical value.

I'm certainly not dismissing the many excellent researchers and fundamental investors out there of course. There are some really skilled people in those areas and they do excellent work. Those who manage to make money over the long run on analyzing news, fundamental and macro factors are highly skilled and usually very specialized. There are two potential issues with that game though. First, it requires some serious research efforts. Large amount of reading, critical thinking and analysis. You need to dig deep into corporate reports and background documentation. Some people like doing that, some don't. It's not an evening exercise, that's for sure.

The other issue is that becoming a skilled fundamental researcher tends to mean a high degree of specialization. This can be a good thing, especially if you focus on an area which becomes the new hot thing. Trouble is, you might be focusing on an area which for some reason becomes a wasteland for a few years, and then you're just out of luck.

It might seem as if the important thing is to find out why a stock is moving, but in reality this is often a futile and unprofitable endeavor. We're not looking for truth here. When it all boils down, we're just looking for money. Any information that can help us in that is welcome. As it turns out, you don't need all that much information. The price itself may be all you need.

Momentum investing is about buying what's moving up. When the price is increasing, we buy in expectation of the share price continuing to increase.

The Rationale behind Momentum Investing

There has been plenty of research as to the causes of momentum returns. It's not very difficult to show that the momentum effect works or at least has worked so far up to now. It's trickier to explain why.

In the academic field, the first influential paper on the subject was published in the 60's (Levy, 1967). Since then there have been some interesting studies confirming their findings and building upon it. One such paper by Jagadeesh and Titman (Jegadeesh & Titman, 1993) came up with two alternative theories as to why momentum investing works.

The first theory was that transactions by investors who buy past winners and sell past losers move the prices away from their long-run values temporarily and thereby causes prices to overreach.

The alternative theory was that the market underreacts to information about the short-term prospects of firms but overreacts to information about their long-term prospects.

There's been plenty of debate on the subject and other theories about why winning stocks tend to keep winning. Possible theories include delayed stock price reactions to common factors, something which Jagadeesh and Titman disagrees with. There's of course the positive feedback cycle of how winning stocks get attention and attract further investors. From a purely practical point of view though, you should ask yourself whether it really matters. If you can show that the momentum effect exists and has produced excess returns in the past, it's likely that it will continue to do so. Speculating in the underlying reasons can be an interesting past time, but is it really relevant to your trading?

There's been plenty of research confirming the momentum effect, both from academics and practitioners and there's not a shortage of well performing equity momentum products. It's hard to argue that momentum investing doesn't work.

When a stock has been heading up a while, it's more likely to keep heading up a bit more than other stocks that didn't have a good run recently.

A crucial point to keep in mind is that the momentum effect will in reality work very differently in a bear market. When we're experiencing bull markets or just regular old boring market conditions, the momentum effect works fine. That's because in normal and good market climates, stocks can move fairly independently from each other. There's a greater focus on the stocks themselves, and less on the overall market.

In a bear market, there's typically an abundance of market level factors. There's usually something that drives the market declines and that will be the deciding factor for more or less all stocks. It could be the collapse of the tech bubble, a global credit meltdown, sovereign defaults or other major events. What happens in bear markets is that all stocks start behaving the same. Diversification becomes an illusion and all stocks move up and down on the same days. The momentum effect isn't very helpful in these kinds of markets.

The Advantage of a Systematic Approach

So let's assume you're with me so far. That I've managed to convince you that momentum investing is a good way to go. The question remains on how to go about it.

One way would be to look at the stocks you know and see which one appears to be moving up. Buy the stocks that are moving up, and don't buy the ones not moving up. The obvious problem is that perhaps the stocks you know are not the most interesting ones. There's no good reason to assume that the stocks you're normally looking at would be the most suitable for momentum investing. The fact that you've followed or even traded these stocks before really doesn't mean anything. They may be the best momentum stocks around, but that's not very likely.

We could also take the chartist route and flip through hundreds of charts, one by one. We'll look at each one to see if it's got positive momentum, short list the strong looking charts and buy the strongest. Even though we expanded the field of view with this approach, it's still not great. There's a substantial discretionary element involved in visually looking at charts. This has the potential of introducing a random element, which can swing either way.

Let's go one step further and use some technical analysis indicators. We could for instance say that we only consider stocks where the 50 day moving average is above the 100 day moving average. It may still leave many stocks to choose from and it doesn't provide a firm guide to which stocks to buy. In the end, even this method may leave a significant discretionary and thereby random element.

Perhaps if we measure the distance between the 50 day moving average and the 100 day moving average. By doing that, we'll have a quantifiable measure of the momentum. We could even make it simpler, and just measure the distance between the price and a moving average. Now compare the percentage distances for a large group of stocks, and you've got a rudimentary ranking method. It's not a great ranking method, but it's a decent start.

Given that we want to build a momentum stock portfolio, we could just start buying from the top of the rankings list until we're filled up. While this helps us in finding the candidate stocks, it's only a part of the whole equation. There are so many questions left to sort out. How much of each stock do you buy? How long do you hold the stocks? When do you replace a stock?

A ranking method is important but it's still just one piece of the strategy. The ranking method is a necessary piece but without a complete strategy you'll still be left with far too many random variables. If you buy the strongest stocks today, then what happens if other stocks are stronger next week or a month from now? You have to have a plan for when to replace your stocks with stronger stocks and under what conditions this is done.

Then there's the critical question of how much of each stock you buy. Lazy methods like spending 5% of your portfolio capital on buying 20 shares won't cut it. Such a simplistic method has many drawbacks, not the least that your portfolio will be driven by the most volatile of your stocks. Another example of random factors.

Earlier I mentioned that it's not a good idea to hold momentum stocks during a bear market. That's an easy statement to make, but it's not as clear how this should be implemented. You need a plan for how and when to increase and decrease your overall portfolio risk. When to buy momentum stocks and when to refrain from buying them.

If you've managed to come up with a plan that covers all these factors, then you have a real trading strategy. The best part is that if you do this correctly, you'll have a quantifiable strategy that can be tested historically. Using careful simulations, you can test what factors have been significant in the past and find what worked and what didn't. This process can help design a solid trading methodology that is highly likely not only to be profitable but to massively outperform the equity markets over time.

The next section of the book will provide you with such a methodology. One that has been tested not only historically but empirically for many years.

6
Market Regime Filter

In chapter 4, I showed some simple trend following style trading models and how they failed to perform satisfactory on stocks. There's a very easy way to significantly improve these models. It's a very simple and straightforward concept and it puzzles me greatly why so many are still not implementing it.

It's very easy: Don't buy stocks in a bear market.

When it comes to trading strategies for stocks, the one indicator that's more important than all the others is the index. At times it may appear as if a stock is independent, moving by its own force, but that's partially an illusion. Almost all stocks are impacted on a daily basis by the overall state of the market. Even a momentum stock backed up by positive news flow and buying pressure is impacted by it. In a bull market, most stocks move up. Momentum stocks are likely to move up more than the others, but most of them move in the same direction.

In a sideways market regime, some stocks move up and some move down. The index may look sideways if you look at a chart covering several months, but on the days it moves up, most stocks perform a little better. Momentum stocks tend to do very well in sideways markets, as long as there's not overly much volatility.

In bear markets, it suddenly doesn't seem to matter which stocks you have anymore. When the overall market index is heading down, almost all stocks follow it. It's just a matter of degree. If you try to search for the strongest stocks of 2008, you'll find that it's practically impossible to find something that was moving up at the time.

When the markets turn down, suddenly everything turns down. Stocks that seemed so independent before are now turning into sheep chased by a dog. In bear markets, correlations quickly start approaching 1 and it doesn't seem to matter much anymore which stocks you've selected. They're all moving down.

If you intend to hold a momentum stock portfolio, or any other stock portfolio for that matter, you always need to be aware of the prevailing market regime.

There are many ways that this could be measured. In the end, it doesn't matter that much which method you pick. It's not that difficult to figure out if the market is in a bull market, sideways market or bear market. Actually, the key thing to figure out is whether or not we're in a bear market. Sideways markets are usually quite good climate to trade momentum strategies.

There's no sense in spending too much time thinking about your exact approach. That's a common mistake by hobby traders, to forget about the objective and focus on the toolbox. Think about what you want to accomplish and find a simple and straight forward way to do it.

In this case, we want to have an indication of the overall market direction in the long run. How could this be done? You could check if the price is above a long term moving average. You could measure the percentage move in past year. Perhaps use a double moving average or a Bollinger band. It's not going to make a whole lot of difference. The critical point is that you need to have a long term market regime indicator.

Since it really doesn't matter much what indicator is used for this, as long as it captures the long term trend of the market, I'm going to use a very simple approach. There's no need to complicate things here.

I'll declare the market to be bearish if the S&P 500 Index is below its 200 day moving average. That's a very long term filter. Using such a simple approach, we immediately have a firm way to identify if the market is in a bear trend or not. Practically all equity portfolio strategies can be improved significantly by simply adding this one rule. If the index is in a bear market, just don't buy stocks.

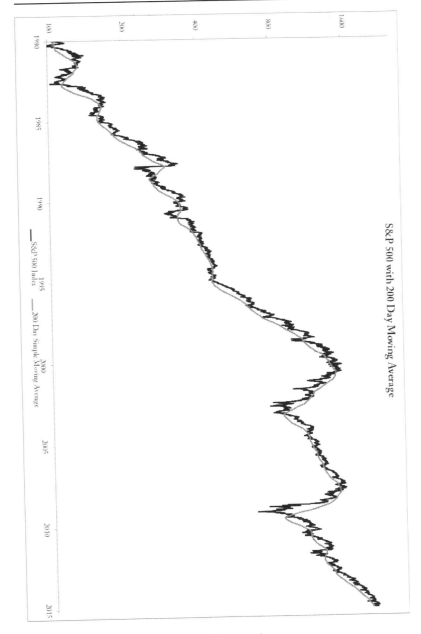

Figure 6-1 S&P 500 Index with 200 day moving average

In Figure 6-1 you'll see the S&P 500 index with a 200 day moving average, since 1980. This picture shows us that most of the time, the index is above this long term average. That's not too surprising. Most of the time, it's a good idea to buy stocks.

Looking at this same figure, you may also notice that many times the index drops down below the moving average, only to quickly jump back up. It would be fair to wonder if it doesn't make sense to do the opposite to what I'm suggesting here. Why not buy when the index moves below the moving average?

That's a whole different type of trading approach. It's a much more difficult one and certainly a riskier one. If you bought right after the 1987 crash, you would have made very good money and quite quickly too. But if you bought after the index breach in 2000, you would find yourself left with only half your money three years later.

No, I'm suggesting something much less risky. The moving average here will be used as an indicator of market regime. It answers one simple question. Is the market heading up? When prices are above the moving average, we'll declare the answer to be affirmative.

Note that in the approach discussed here, the index and its moving average has no direct implication on trading. It doesn't tell you to buy or to sell. We don't sell just because the index moved down below the moving average. But, and here is the important part, we don't allow any new positions when the index is below its long term moving average.

Don't buy stocks in a bear market.

7

Ranking Stocks

When you're dealing with a large set of possible instruments to trade, it becomes important to find a good way to rank them. If you're looking at the constituent stocks of the S&P 500, you can't start picking stocks at random. Well, chapter 15 shows that perhaps you can, but that's a later story. Buying the ones you're familiar with or read about in the newspaper is even worse. Don't even think about clicking through 500 charts to find the patterns you like. That'll leave you at the mercy of your visual perception and no matter how much you try to be consistent, you're very likely to make different calls on different days. Your mood, attention span and other factors will play in and you won't get consistent results.

The first thing you need to do is to figure out what you want to capture. While the core scope of this book is about momentum, the principles can be used for other styles as well. That should be a good area of research for you, if you like this book and the ideas it presents.

Momentum is essentially about buying the stocks that gain the most. So we'll just rank the stocks based on their gains, right? Well, as much as I'm in favor of simple solutions, this may be a little too simple. It's important to understand why that is the case.

Take a very common ranking method found on various internet websites. A popular method seems to be to rank by the percent difference between the price and a moving average. For a long term ranking, this could be the percent difference between the current price and a 200 day moving average. There are two main problems with this kind of approach.

First, it doesn't take the normal volatility of the stock into account at all. That will lead to selecting very high volatility stocks where it's just business as usual for them to run far away from the moving average and fall back down again. Second and more importantly, this method doesn't care about how we came to be far above the moving average. If there was a massive event that moved the price very far in a single day, such as a potential takeover, that would push the stock to the top of the rankings.

Volatility is very important. This game isn't about who makes the highest absolute return in a year. It's about who has the most return per unit of volatility. Never forget that volatility is the currency that we use to buy performance. What we want to achieve is to pay as little volatility as possible for as much performance as we can get. Simply looking at returns without the risk side is strictly in the realm of gambling and that's not what we're doing here.

This leads to the obvious conclusion that we need to find stocks that move up in a nice and orderly fashion. We want stocks that not only show significant gains over time, but move as smoothly as possible. Therefore we need two building blocks for our ranking method. We need to take both the momentum and the volatility into account.

Let's first find a good way to measure the momentum by itself. That's really not that difficult, and more a matter of preference. Try to avoid the all too common reaction of looking at the usual suspects of technical analysis tools. I find that many hobby traders tend to get stuck in a way of thinking, based on the myriad of technical analysis books that have been published for the past few decades. Many of these tools were made in a different era for different purposes. Try to start from scratch and design analytics for your own purpose, without using the usual technical analysis terminology. Even if you end up using something similar, at least it's a good exercise. It will give you a deeper understanding of the methods, as opposed to using canned technical analysis indicators.

I prefer my analytics to be based on decent math and logic, make intuitive sense and preferably be easy to visualize if need be. Your method of choice may be different than mine and that's just fine. What's important is that you find something that fits your purpose. If you make up your own analytic, be sure to do some proper simulation work to ensure that it actually adds value.

Using Exponential Regression for Ranking Stocks

My usual method of ranking stocks may for some seem overly complex. It really isn't, once you get past the basic statistic calculations involved. If you find this section complex, my first advice would be to take your time to try to understand the logic behind it. For those with limited prior exposure to statistical analysis, the formulas and terminology may appear much more complex than they really are. Trust me, this isn't scary.

If you still find these concepts too complex, feel free to replace them with your own method of choice. Look at the logic and what we're trying to achieve and find something simpler that can get the job done. I'll do my best to try to explain the methods I'm using and why I've settled on them.

For measuring momentum, I use exponential regression. This opens the two obvious questions, what is regression and why is it exponential. Before looking at the exponential part, you need to understand the concept of linear regression. I'm not going too much into formulas and details, and this discussion will be kept on a cursory level. My apologies to fellow quants who may feel that this explanation is overly simplified.

Linear regression is a method of fitting a line over a series of values. It's a way of finding the best fitting line, in this case to a time series of prices. Figure 7-1 shows an example, where a linear regression line has been fitted over the price series. Note that this is not a trend line. A trend line is something very subjective and can be drawn in many different ways. We're talking about a linear regression line, calculated based on the price points.

Figure 7-1 shows a linear regression line calculated on Microsoft in the late 90s. The linear regression formulas will give you two values which are needed to draw a regression line like this. First you can calculate the intercept, i.e. where to start drawing the line. Then you have the slope, which tells you how much the line should move up or down for each successive data point. The resulting line is the best linear fit to the price data, or rather the one with the least errors.

The slope is what really interests us, since that's what tells us the direction of the stock price.

For daily data, the slope will tell us how many dollars and cents the line should move up or down per day. This is after all, as the name implies a straight line. Calculating the linear regression slope on a daily price series is therefore the same as calculating the average incline or decline per day over the same time period.

The linear regression slope is therefore a measure of the speed, or momentum of the stock. The problem however is that the slope is expressed in dollars and cents. If a stock that's priced at $10 moves up by two dollars per day, that's more significant than if a stock priced at $100 advances by the same two dollars each day.

This is the reason for using exponential regression. While the linear regression slope is expressed in currency units, the exponential slope is expressed in percent. The exponential regression slope will tell you how many percent, up or down, the line moves. Or if you prefer, the average percentage move per day.

Obviously this slope number will normally have many decimals and be hard to relate to. Most stocks don't have slopes over a percent, or even half a percent. After all, if a stock had a slope of one percent per day, it would imply that it moves over 200% in a year. Instead, you'll end up with slopes such as 0.000435 and other numbers that are difficult to make sense of and to relate to. The easy solution to this is to annualize it.

If you annualize the slope, you get a number that tells you how much, in theory, the stock would gain in a full year if it continued the exact same angle.

Not that you can make any sort of assumption that this will happen, because it probably won't. The reason is just to get a number easier to relate to. If you see that the exponential regression slope is 0.0006 that's tough to relate to, but if you're told that this implies 16% on an annualized basis, that's easier to understand.

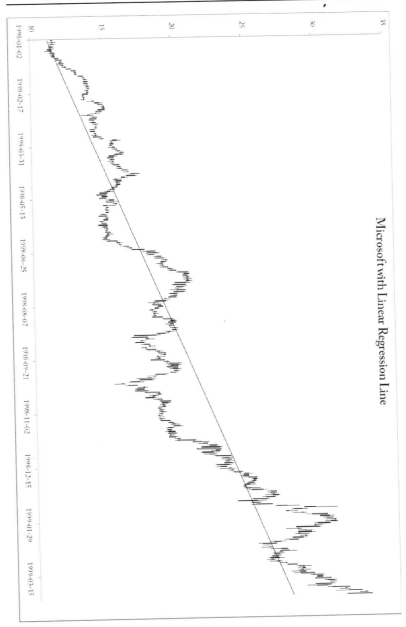

Figure 7-1 Linear Regression Line, Microsoft

The concept is more important than the math, but let's briefly look at how this 16% number came about. First we calculated the exponential regression slope of the stock. That can be done using most standard charting packages or in a spreadsheet application like Excel.

The exponential slope in this hypothetical case ended up at 0.0006. That means that on an average day, the stock moves up by 0.06% per day. Assuming 250 trading days in a year, it's very easy to annualize this.

$$1.16178 = (1 + 0.0006)^{250}$$

Simple financial math tells us that 0.06% gains compounded for 250 days will end up at about 16% in a year. Now the number makes more intuitive sense.

Thinking in terms of percent is much more helpful than thinking in terms of dollars and cents. After all, it's not very useful to know that Stock XYZ gained $30 in the past week. It really says nothing without context. If however that same stock gained 30% last week, now that has to be significant.

As mentioned, a neat part with this method of using annualized exponential regression slope is that it makes intuitive sense. We can see how many percent per year the current slope represents. The important part to remember is that we don't actually expect that this return will realize. It could be much smaller or much larger. What it does is to put the recent past into perspective, in a way that we can relate to.

In this book, we're looking for a medium term momentum ranking. The regression calculations are all done using the past 90 trading days. This makes for a reasonable time period without resorting to optimizations.

When the line in the lower pane is above zero, the stock is heading up, else it's heading down. The higher the number, the stronger is the momentum.

If we now calculate the exponential regression slope for all the stocks we're considering, annualize the numbers and sort them based on the resulting value, we've got a pretty good ranking method. Not a perfect one, but a pretty good one.

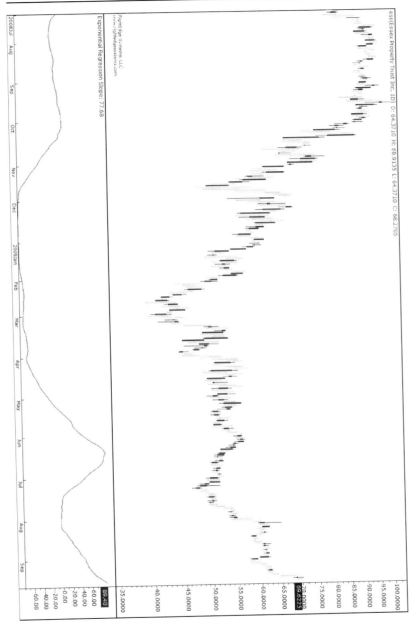

Figure 7-2 Essex Property Trust, Annualized Exp. Regression Slope

Figure 7-2 shows Essex Property Trust with the bottom chart being the annualized exponential regression slope. Note the zero level on the scale.

The stock with the highest slope will be on top of the list. The stronger something is moving up, the higher up the list. This is a pure momentum ranking.

There is still one little problem with our ranking approach. Using just annualized exponential regression for ranking means that we don't care about the fit. If for instance a stock has gone sideways for a couple of months, then suddenly make a single day move up of 50% only to continue to go sideways again, that would really mess with our ranking. Impossible you say? Not at all. That's a normal behavior for a stock that announces an imminent takeover. The price quickly jumps up very close to the takeover price before losing all volatility and heading sideways until the deal is complete. That's not the kind of situation that we want to buy. You can probably imagine more odd scenarios that can happen.

We don't want to pick a stock that just had a massive jump. We want to get stocks that had as smooth ride as possible. Preferably we want to get stocks that continue in a very smooth ascent after we buy them too. We're looking for real momentum stocks, not stocks that just had crazy gaps.

Observant readers have already noticed the hint dropped a couple of paragraphs ago about the solution. The operative word here being 'fit'. Since we're using regression math, there's a perfectly fine method to measure how well our price data fits the regression line. It's called coefficient of determination, usually designated R^2.

The R^2 tells you how well the price series fits the regression line. If you have a bunch of random price points all over the place, you can still calculate a regression line. The result will of course be nonsense, since there's no connection between those dots. No actual slope to be predicted. In that case, the R^2 will be close to zero.

If on the other hand the real data is already almost a completely straight line, we'll get the opposite result. If we're calculating a regression slope based on price data that's moving up in an almost perfect line, we can expect to get an R^2 reading of near 1.

Zero is the minimum value for the R^2 while one is the maximum. A value of one means that the data is a perfect fit to the line, and the lower the R^2, the worse the fit of the regression line. Again, remember that an understanding of the logic is much more important than knowing all the formulas.

And now for the quiz of the day. Given the two values we've now got at our disposal, how can we make a better ranking? We've got the annualized slope of the stock and we've got a number between 0 and 1 that tells us how well that line fits reality.

Yes, that's right. Let's just multiply these guys and see what we get. If the fit of the regression line is low, we'll bring the number down. If the fit is high, it won't get pushed down much. What this means is that we measure the pure momentum, in the regression slope, and then we punish it for volatility. The higher the volatility, the worse the punishment.

What you'll find is that for the most part, the ranking list will look quite similar. The difference is that the stocks with the most extreme fits, good or bad, will make large shifts in rank. The largest impact is that the stocks that made substantial gains under massive volatility will be pushed far down the list, far enough to be off the realistic candidates. That's exactly what we want to achieve with using the R^2 fitness method.

Figure 7-3 shows the annualized exponential regression slope in the middle pane. That's the pure momentum, the annualized regression slope. The bottom pane is the fit, the coefficient of determination. Lastly, you see the two multiplied.

Note how the R^2 drops down fast when volatility increases. When the price moves in a reasonably smooth trend, like you see in the middle of Figure 7-3, the R^2 will remain quite high. In that case, the momentum ranking doesn't get punished very much. On the other hand, when the price is changing direction or becoming erratic, the R^2 will drop down and thereby pull the adjusted ranking down with it.

This way, our momentum rankings will be a combination of momentum, in the form of the regression slope, and also a quality measurement in terms of the R^2. Multiply the exponential regression slope by the coefficient of determination (R^2) and you have a pretty good basis to rank stocks against each other.

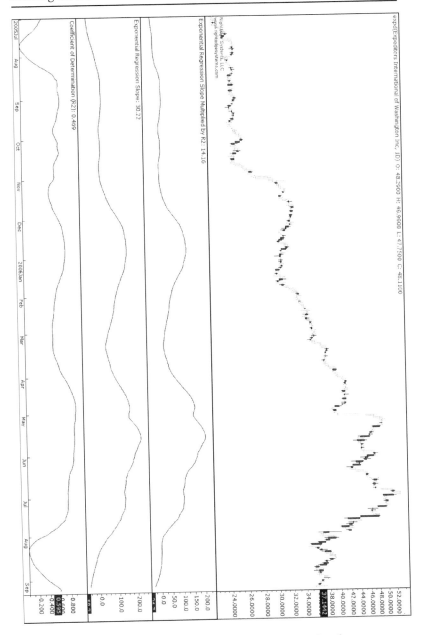

Figure 7-3 Regression Slope and Fit, Expeditors International

Although Excel is hardly a practical environment to perform all these ranking calculations, it might still be useful to do it once manually in a spreadsheet application. It's not practical to use Excel for automating these tables, but it could help to understand the logic better.

Figure 7-4 demonstrates how to calculate the adjusted slope in Excel. This is the number that we'll use to rank all the stocks for this momentum strategy. What this does is simply to make a log series from the price and apply standard regression formulas on it. Nothing else.

The first column shows number of days since the start of the time series. Second column is the date and third is the price. So far, no actual calculations.

In column D, the natural logarithm of the price is calculated. This is our basis for exponential regression calculations. Column E is a standard Excel Slope() formula, to calculate the regression slope of the log series.

To arrive at an annualized return in column F, we need to convert the slope back by applying the Exp() function. That gives us the percentage change per day in the slope. Now annualize that by raising it to the power of 250 trading days and you've got your percentage.

Calculate the R^2 using the RSQ() function, multiply with the slope and voila.

What this all will result in is a list of all the stocks in your selected universe, ranked on adjusted slope. In this case, the universe was the S&P 500 stocks. In Table 7-1 you'll see a ranking of the top 30 stocks in the S&P 500, as of writing this. The actual top stocks changes all the time of course and this list is outdated by the time you read it.

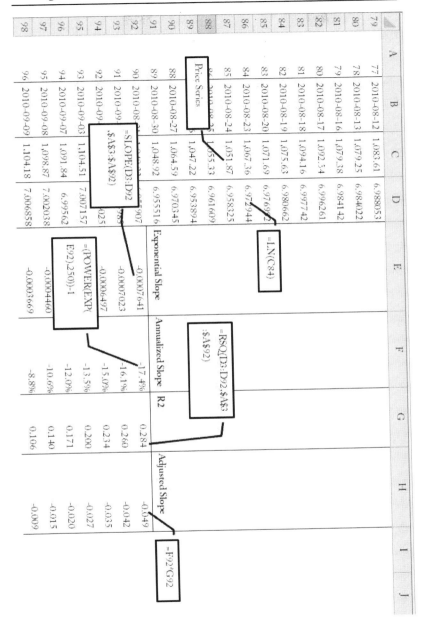

Figure 7-4 Regression Logic in Excel

Table 7-1 Top Stocks Ranking

Rank	Ticker	Name	Sector	Adjusted Slope	ATR	Target Weight
1	SPLS	Staples Inc	Consumer Discretionary	257.94	0.70	2.4%
2	EA	Electronic Arts Inc	Information Technology	240.75	1.53	3.6%
3	MAC	Macerich Co	Financials	177.92	1.59	5.5%
4	WFM	Whole Foods Market Inc	Consumer Staples	174.24	1.20	4.4%
5	WHR	Whirlpool Corp	Consumer Discretionary	156.52	5.14	4.0%
6	AVGO	Avago Technologies Ltd	Information Technology	147.28	3.66	2.9%
7	LOW	Lowe's Companies Inc	Consumer Discretionary	144.55	1.44	5.0%
8	KR	Kroger Co	Consumer Staples	143.62	1.05	6.8%
9	KMX	Carmax Inc	Consumer Discretionary	138.51	1.42	4.6%
10	LUV	Southwest Airlines Co	Industrials	137.14	1.53	2.9%
11	GLW	Corning Inc	Information Technology	132.43	0.58	4.3%
12	HSP	Hospira Inc	Health Care	130.84	2.14	4.1%
13	GGP	General Growth Properties Inc	Financials	126.00	0.54	5.5%
14	SHW	Sherwin-Williams Co	Materials	124.95	4.83	5.8%
15	PCG	PG&E Corp	Utilities	120.13	1.13	5.0%
16	STZ	Constellation Brands Inc	Consumer Staples	116.21	2.03	5.6%
17	LB	L Brands Inc	Consumer Discretionary	115.18	2.03	4.6%
18	DAL	Delta Air Lines Inc	Industrials	113.50	1.67	2.7%
19	MHK	Mohawk Industries Inc	Consumer Discretionary	108.91	3.68	4.6%
20	DLTR	Dollar Tree Inc	Consumer Discretionary	106.75	1.69	4.5%
22	NOC	Northrop Grumman Corp	Industrials	106.64	3.02	5.5%

23	SCG	SCANA Corp	Utilities	103.42	1.16	5.3%
24	PNW	Pinnacle West Capital Corp	Utilities	101.75	1.25	5.4%
25	HCN	Health Care REIT Inc	Financials	100.14	1.49	5.2%
26	TGT	Target Corp	Consumer Discretionary	99.44	1.60	4.8%
27	SEE	Sealed Air Corp	Materials	95.83	1.13	4.0%
28	BXP	Boston Properties Inc	Financials	94.80	2.26	6.3%
29	DRI	Darden Restaurants Inc	Consumer Discretionary	93.55	1.08	5.7%
30	PDCO	Patterson Companies Inc	Health Care	93.36	0.90	5.5%

The key columns are the three last ones. The adjusted slope is simply the annualized exponential regression slope, multiplied by the R^2. The next column is the ATR reading, in this case based on a 20 day period. Finally there's a calculation of the target weight for the stock, should it be included in your portfolio. This is a very easy, but still very important calculation and that will be covered in detail in chapter 8, which deals with position sizes.

So how do you construct a portfolio from this? It's really easy.

Start buying from the top of the list, until you run out of cash. That's how you make your initial portfolio. With this current list, we'll be able to buy the first 23 stocks before running out of cash. The position sizes are calculated to approximate risk parity, i.e. to allocate the same risk to each position. As each stock has different volatility, that means allocating different amount of cash to them each. More on that later in chapter 8.

Just picking the top stocks sounds risky, some might point out. What if we get 25 biotech stocks? Well, if you're really concerned about that you might want to add a sector cap. But you should know that nothing near such extreme portfolios have ever come up, either in simulations or in my own experience of managing such portfolios with real money. Figure 7-5 shows the sector allocation for this approach as of February 2015. It's not an index portfolio for sure, but there's nothing odd with it. In fact, it's quite logical. There are no energy stocks, as that sector has been taking a severe beating for over half a year. There are no telecom stocks, as that sector has been dead for longer than anyone can remember. It's overweighted in discretionary and staples, two sectors that had been doing very well at this time.

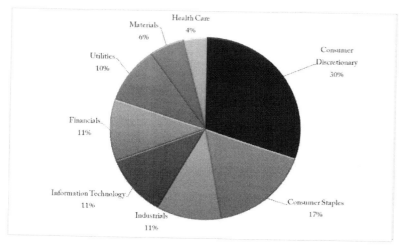

Figure 7-5 Sector Allocation, Sample Initial Portfolio

All in all, it's the kind of portfolio that a skilled fundamental analyst might have constructed. It's a portfolio I would be perfectly comfortable with and not lose any sleep over.

Additional Filters

The ranking method described above works well on its own. However, I prefer to add two more criteria for a stock to be considered. They're very simple and logical.

First, a stock must be trading above its 100 day moving average to be considered a buy candidate. If it's not, it's really not a momentum situation. In normal markets, any stock near the top part of the momentum ranking will be trading far above its 100 day moving average. This rule just makes sure that you don't buy stocks that are moving sideways or down, just because there are no available stocks moving up. Such a situation could otherwise develop in a bear market and especially when the market is just turning from bull to bear. So any stock trading below the 100 day moving average is disqualified.

Second, gaps make me nervous. If there has been any move larger than 15% in the past 90 days, the stock is also disqualified. If you include these situations, there's a risk that you end up getting stocks that are not really momentum situations. Short term shocks may have caused the stock to move significantly, at times even enough to push the volatility adjusted momentum ranking very high. We want long term developments, not sudden gaps.

So the ranking method is then:

- Annualized 90 day exponential regression, multiplied by coefficient of determination.
- Only consider stocks that are above the 100 day moving average.
- Disqualify any stock that has a move larger than 15% in the past 90 days.

8
Position Size

So you've decided which stock to buy. That's a good step in the right direction. But now you're faced with a very important, but often neglected decision. The size of your position and how it changes over time can make all the difference in the world.

When it comes to position size, you need to remember that we're not allocating money. We're allocating risk. That's the key to understanding position sizing. The amount of cash used is not a critical factor. That might be a limiting factor when dealing in cash instruments such a stocks, since you pay for these instruments in full and leverage is expensive. It's not however a guiding factor when it comes to position sizing.

It's important to understand why it's a bad idea to think in terms of cash allocation. This is a very common mistake made not only by the vast majority of retail traders and investors but also by a large amount of fund and asset managers. It's appealing to use such methods because it's so simple.

A classic approach is to aim for having 20 stocks in your portfolio, and simply buying 5% of each. Holding around 20 stocks seems like a good number for achieving reasonable diversification and on the surface this idea might appear to be a good plan. The problem is that this introduces a random variable to your risk and it tilts your portfolio towards the most volatile issues.

If all your stocks have more or less identical volatility, then this equal weight approach should work just fine. That's not likely to be the case in reality though. Some stocks tend to move up or down by half a percent per day while others tend to have daily average moves of over 2%. If you combine such stocks in the same portfolio and allocate equal amount of cash, you're letting the volatile stocks take charge. The overall profits or gains of your portfolio will be highly dependent on a few volatile stocks, while the performance of the less volatile stocks won't matter very much.

Let's make a real life momentum stock portfolio and see how the composition would differ, using a cash allocation approach and a risk allocation approach. The stocks below are, as of writing this, some of the top momentum performers in the S&P 500. By the time this goes to print, that will of course be very outdated. In the first portfolio version, we use the old fashion method of allocating an equal amount of cash to each stock. We just spend the same amount of money on each and every one of them, completely disregarding volatility.

Table 8-1 Simple equal weighted portfolio

Ticker	Name	Sector	Equal Weight
SPLS	Staples Inc	Consumer Discretionary	5%
EA	Electronic Arts Inc	Information Technology	5%
MAC	Macerich Co	Financials	5%
WFM	Whole Foods Market Inc	Consumer Staples	5%
WHR	Whirlpool Corp	Consumer Discretionary	5%
KMX	Carmax Inc	Consumer Discretionary	5%
DAL	Delta Air Lines Inc	Industrials	5%
LUV	Southwest Airlines Co	Industrials	5%
KR	Kroger Co	Consumer Staples	5%
LB	L Brands Inc	Consumer Discretionary	5%
DLTR	Dollar Tree Inc	Consumer Discretionary	5%
HSP	Hospira Inc	Health Care	5%
STZ	Constellation Brands Inc	Consumer Staples	5%
LEG	Leggett & Platt Inc	Consumer Discretionary	5%
TGT	Target Corp	Consumer Discretionary	5%

VTR	Ventas Inc	Financials	5%
CELG	Celgene Corp	Health Care	5%
ROST	Ross Stores Inc	Consumer Discretionary	5%
PDCO	Patterson Companies Inc	Health Care	5%
MNST	Monster Beverage Corp	Consumer Staples	5%

This seems like a well balanced portfolio of well-known companies, diversified over many sectors. There are good reasons why some sectors are missing. Energy for instance has been a terribly underperforming sector since the crude oil price started plummeting in mid-2014. There are also no utilities or telecom stocks, as these are sectors that have been out of favor for some time and the same goes for the materials sector.

Note that the sector composition here is not by design. No discretionary decisions were made in that regard. The portfolio was merely constructed by picking the top momentum stocks on a particular day.

The stocks selected make for a good momentum portfolio at the time. They're chosen based on valid momentum criteria. The weights however can be improved. Some of these stocks are much more volatile than the others. If we allocate an equal amount of cash to each, we'll get a portfolio which will be dominated by these more volatile issues. On any normal market day, the portfolio will mostly be impacted by these stocks and not by the others. By allocating equal notional weight, we have created a very unbalanced portfolio.

The solution to this is quite simple really. It's an approach usually referred to as risk parity allocation. By looking at the volatility of each stock, we can scale each position size according to that. The idea is to buy smaller positions of volatile stocks, so that each stock has an equal theoretical ability to impact the bottom line of the portfolio.

Table 8-2 shows what the weights would look like if we take the volatility into account. Note that all calculations are based on market data as it was at the time of writing. The numbers are therefore outdated by the time you read this.

Table 8-2 Risk parity sized portfolio

Ticker	Name	Sector	Risk Parity Weight
SPLS	Staples Inc	Consumer Discretionary	3.5%
EA	Electronic Arts Inc	Information Technology	4.1%
MAC	Macerich Co	Financials	6.2%
WFM	Whole Foods Market Inc	Consumer Staples	5.1%
WHR	Whirlpool Corp	Consumer Discretionary	5.0%
KMX	Carmax Inc	Consumer Discretionary	4.8%
DAL	Delta Air Lines Inc	Industrials	3.1%
LUV	Southwest Airlines Co	Industrials	3.1%
KR	Kroger Co	Consumer Staples	7.6%
LB	L Brands Inc	Consumer Discretionary	5.3%
DLTR	Dollar Tree Inc	Consumer Discretionary	4.8%
HSP	Hospira Inc	Health Care	5.5%
STZ	Constellation Brands Inc	Consumer Staples	6.1%
LEG	Leggett & Platt Inc	Consumer Discretionary	5.3%
TGT	Target Corp	Consumer Discretionary	5.1%
VTR	Ventas Inc	Financials	6.7%
CELG	Celgene Corp	Health Care	3.4%
ROST	Ross Stores Inc	Consumer Discretionary	5.2%
PDCO	Patterson Companies Inc	Health Care	6.4%
MNST	Monster Beverage Corp	Consumer Staples	3.6%

As you see, there's quite some variation in the risk parity based sizes. The smallest stock only has a weight of 3.1%, while the largest is 7.6%. This reflects that Southwest Airlines is considerably more volatile than Kroger. We don't want to buy much more risk of LUV just because it tends to move more. Buying an equal dollar amount of these two stocks doesn't make any sense, unless of course you really want to take on a much larger risk in the airline.

When it comes to position sizing for investment strategies such equity momentum, the exact details aren't what's important. It's not whether you buy 3.4% or 3.6% of Celgene. The important part is the concept and getting the implementation more or less ok. If you understand the reasoning why it's a bad idea to allocate the same amount of cash to all stocks, then you've come a long way in solving your position sizing. A dollar in one stock isn't the same risk as a dollar in the next stock and the normal volatility of each stock needs to be taken into account.

The method used in Table 8-2 is very simple and easy for anyone to implement. There are considerably more complicated methods used by industry professionals, but the marginal value isn't very high. For those who already have expensive tools at their fingertips, using complicated methods is easy and doesn't hurt. But the bulk of the benefits of risk parity sizing can be had with the simple formula here.

$$Shares = \frac{AccountValue * RiskFactor}{ATR}$$

ATR in this equation stands for Average True Range. It's a common measure of how much an instrument tends to move on an average day, up or down. The true range is just the maximum of the day's high to low or move from previous day. The ATR therefore is just an average of these figures for a number of days back. How many days to use is a matter of preference and purpose and not overwhelmingly important. I used 20 days for the calculations in Table 8-2. The ATR can be easily calculated or even found automatically in most financial software applications.

Risk factor is an arbitrary number that sets a target daily impact for the stock. If you set this number to 0.001, then you're targeting a daily impact on the portfolio of 0.1%, or 10 basis points. Assuming of course that the ATR stays on more or less the same level as in the recent past.

The lower you set the risk factor, the smaller the position size of the stock will be. The implication of this in the context of building stock portfolios is clear. The lower the risk factor, the higher the number of stocks you'll get. This is because we'll keep buying until we run out of cash, and with a lower risk factor each stock will use up less cash.

Therefore, the diversification will increase as we lower the risk factor. Just remember that in equity world, diversification only helps you to a certain point. There's a clear advantage in diversification from holding ten stocks instead of five, but it's questionable if there's any value in holding 40 stocks instead of 30.

As an example of how to calculate position size using this approach, let's look at Monster Beverages. Figure 8-1 shows the price chart of this company along with a 20 day ATR at the bottom. If we were to buy this stock, we can use the latest ATR reading for our position sizing formula. The last reading is 3.26, meaning that on average, this stock has had a daily range of 3.26 USD for the past 20 days. On an average day, that's how much this stock tends to move. A reasonable risk factor might be 10 basis points, or 0.1%. Remember that this is arbitrary and that a higher number will mean fewer stocks with larger size.

Let's further assume that our entire trading account is worth $100,000. So how many shares of Monster do we buy?

$$\frac{100,000 * 0.001}{3.26} = 30 \ Shares$$

The numerator in this equation is our target daily impact. 100,000 multiplied by 0.001 is 100. This is an important number here. What we're trying to achieve with this formula is for each stock in our portfolio to move on average 100 dollars per day, up or down. The amount $100 is 10 basis points of our portfolio, and that's how much we want each stock to impact the portfolio on a daily basis.

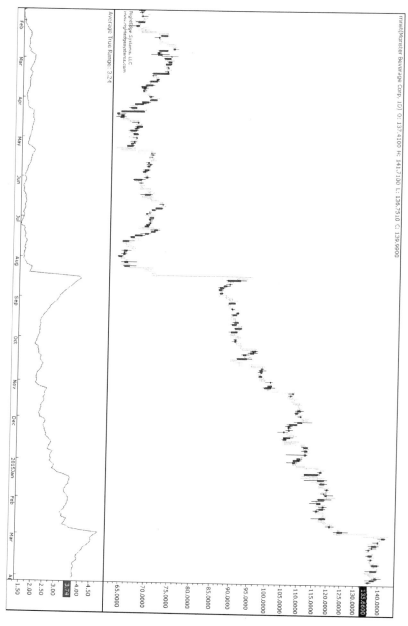

Figure 8-1 Monster Beverage, with 20 day ATR

Since this particular stock tends to move in a range of $3.26 per day, we therefore need to divide our target move for the position with the average daily move for this stock. Divide 100 by 3.26 and you arrive at 30.67. Let's round that down and buy 30 shares.

The current share price is 118.93, so buying 30 of those will cost $3,567.90. That in turn means that the portfolio weight of this position will be $3,567.90 divided by $100,000, which is of course 3.57%.

Always remember that when allocating position size, we're allocating risk and not cash. We look at the volatility of the stock and set the size based on that. Let the cash allocation land where it may.

Position Rebalancing

This is a very important topic. If you come from the institutional world, you'll think this is so obvious that it doesn't even need to be said, not alone have its own section. After all, this is something that most people in the business do regular as clockwork at certain intervals. Naturally you need to rebalance, or you'll end up unbalanced.

If you didn't work in institutional asset management however, this may be something new that could potentially make a large impact on your long term results. Rebalancing is about how you change your position size over time. And no, I don't mean how you double the size on success or how you double down when you lose. Those types of activities are strictly gambling. Rebalance is about changing your position size to get it back to where you set it in the first place.

Remember how I explained in the previous section that when you size positions, you allocate risk and not cash? Well, risk changes over time. It's not a very static factor.

To really understand rebalancing you must first have a full understanding of volatility based position sizing. While there are different variations of this concept, we'll use the ATR based formula presented earlier since it does the job well and is very easy to implement without expensive risk tools.

There is however one glaring problem. Something which far too many people overlook. Observant readers should already have spotted the problem in Figure 8-1. Do you see it?

The obvious issue is that volatility isn't stationary. For Monster Beverages, the ATR was moving around $1.5 for most of 2014, only to suddenly make a massive jump up to $3.8 in August. Then it fell back down to around $2 before slowly moving up to a little over $3.

If we had bought this stock in July 2014, we would have calculated a very different size than if we bought in early 2015. Using the July 2014 data, and the same initial portfolio size, we would end up with the following calculation.

$$\frac{100,000 * 0.001}{1.56} = 64 \; Shares$$

Yes, we would have bought more than double the number of shares if we had bought in July. The initial theoretical risk would be about the same. As the share price moves along, our position risk changes rather dramatically. If we held those shares into early 2015, we would now have over double the risk level that we were trying to target. Now we would be experiencing an average daily impact of over 20 basis points, whereas we had tried to target 10.

Then there's one more non-static variable in this equation, namely the total portfolio value. Not only is this impacted by the performance of this position over time, it's also impacted by the performance of other positions. Add to that the potential inflows and outflows of your portfolio, if you're managing money for others or if you add or decrease your portfolio on your own.

Even if nothing happens to your position, the risk can still change. If for instance other positions in your portfolio have great success, making big gains, then suddenly your static position will have a much lower risk allocation than it should. The portfolio value went up because of the performance of the other stocks, and now all your position size calculations are off.

The same of course if other positions are experiencing large losses. As you see, position sizing is something that has to be viewed from a dynamic point of view. It's not a fire-and-forget type of solution.

This all means that your position sizes need to be regularly reviewed and rebalanced. You need to change the position size in order for it to stay the same. For the approximate risk allocation to stay the same, you need to keep changing the number of shares you own.

Going back to the Monster chart in Figure 8-1, if we bought the shares in July, we would absolutely need to change the size in August. In this case, we need to sell quite a lot of shares. Perhaps at this point someone is asking about 'letting the profits run'. After all, it's a common expression that means that you should never sell a winning position. Well, these mantras are quite useless in the first place. Real life isn't simple enough to be boiled down to a few punchy quotes.

Here, we are letting the position stay in, but allowing the risk allocation run wild without any control is as irrational as it is irresponsible. Professionals rebalance their positions for a reason.

It's advisable to rebalance all position sizes on a regular basis. For longer term investment strategies such as equity momentum portfolios, a bi-weekly or monthly frequency is good enough. There's usually no point in doing this on a daily basis, as it would greatly increase trading volume and transaction costs.

To reduce trading volume, you could set a filter for how much difference between target risk and current risk there has to be for a rebalance action to occur. That would prevent you from doing too many smaller trades on each rebalancing day.

You may also want to trigger a rebalance straight away for stocks when they have extraordinary moves. In the case of the Monster Beverage example, such an event would be the dramatic jump in price in mid-August 2014, as can be seen in the Figure 8-1.

9
When to Sell

I bet you're wondering about the stop loss logic. What it's based on, how far away it is, whether the stop loss order is placed in the market or triggered on closing prices.

Well, sorry to disappoint you. There are no stop losses here.

Some types of trading strategies require the use of stop loss orders, while others don't. Momentum stock portfolios don't need this. In fact, using stop loss logic for this type of strategy will most likely show an adverse effect. There are better ways to decide when to kick out a stock.

Trend followers normally use a trailing stop. That means that you stay in a position as long as it doesn't move down a certain distance. This is valid exit method for some types of strategies. Always keep in mind the underlying logic of things. It's a very common trap to fall into worn old mantras about how to let profits run, cutting losses, letting the trend be your friend until it bends and such. Don't get stuck in these mantras. The fact of the matter is that sometimes these things may be true and sometimes they are not. What you need is to apply common sense and critical thinking, not old quotes taken out of context. And you can quote me on that.

If we were to construct a portfolio based on the ranking concept presented in chapter 7 and then employ trailing stop logic, we would have a very obvious problem. A stock could continue to move sideways forever, and we would still be holding it. Given the problem of limited cash that we face when trading stocks, that's a real concern.

Even if the stock keeps moving up, perhaps there are other stocks moving up much more. A trailing stop wouldn't kick that stock out just because it underperforms the peers. After a while, we would end up with an old and stale portfolio with underperforming stocks.

Remember how we first put the portfolio together. It was based on the best performing stocks in the universe we cover. Wouldn't it make much more sense if we base our exit criteria on the same logic?

This brings us to the very important topic of portfolio rebalancing.

Portfolio Rebalancing

In the previous chapter I described the importance of position rebalancing. This entails recalculating all position sizes and making sure that they still have the same risk allocation as they did when they were initiated. As volatility changes, position sizes need to be regularly adjusted to match.

On the portfolio level, you have a similar task to perform on a regular basis. This involves checking if the stocks you're holding are fulfilling the criteria needed for them to remain in your portfolio.

Remember the ranking tables we looked at in chapter 7. These tables will show us the current top stocks, based on the adjusted slope concept described there. By sorting the stocks on this slope, you'll get a rank for each stock, from 1 for the best and getting higher and higher the worse the slope is.

The exact rank for any given stock will vary day by day, so once we bought a stock we have to give it a little leeway. If for instance we hold a portfolio of around 20 stocks and require that a stock must remain in the top 30, that would mean far too much trading activity and we would keep selling perfectly fine momentum stocks.

We could however say that when we perform the portfolio rebalance, each stock in the portfolio must be in the top 20% of the stocks in the S&P 500, or whatever your investment universe is, for it to remain in the portfolio.

The exact cutoff can vary. If you have a very wide stock universe, the S&P 1500 for instance, then you could set a lower cutoff. You could require the stock to be in the top 10% or even 5%. The point is the logic. Instead of having a stop loss level, we keep a stock for as long as it remains one of the very strongest stocks available.

But what if all stocks are moving down? Yes, that's a real concern. So we have to have another criterion too. A failsafe. Let's keep that real simple and just add a trend indicator.

Let's kick our stocks out of the portfolio if they are no longer in the top 20% of the stocks in our investment universe, or if it's trading below its 100 day moving average.

Such simple exit criteria are actually quite sufficient and will work just fine. No need for trailing stops or similar.

The second task in portfolio rebalancing is to figure out what to do with the cash after we sell a stock. Perhaps a stock just fell out of the top 20% or dropped below its 100 day moving average. We sell it, and we're left with a pile of cash. Now what?

The circle simply repeats. First check the market regime filter. Is the index trading above its 200 day moving average? If it's not, you're not allowed to buy. Yes, this means that you've got an automatic exposure scale-out. This is a key part of this entire strategy. If the index drops below its trend filter, we don't replace stocks when they are sold. We don't sell just because the index went bearish, but we don't buy new stocks either. This will result in a slow and orderly scale out of positions.

If the index level is all green, we check the top list again. Make a new table of the top momentum stocks, using the adjusted slope concept shown in chapter 7. Pick the top stocks from the list. Buy the highest ranked stocks in the list that we don't already own, until you're out of cash.

No discretionary decisions are needed. You never have to stop and wonder about what to do. The rules are very clear and that helps you perform in the long run.

The portfolio rebalancing should be done more often than the position rebalancing. You could for instance do the portfolio rebalancing every week, looking for stocks to sell and replace, and then only to the position size rebalancing once or twice per month.

10

A Complete Momentum Trading Strategy

Now that we've talked about the necessary building blocks for a real strategy, we're ready to construct a solid set of rules. Having rigid trading rules offers great advantages. You'll always have a set course of action. Your decisions will never be based on randomness or your mood of the day. In case of market distress, you'll have a ready plan that you know has worked in the past.

When you have a solid set of rules you will be able to relax more. It's much easier to have confidence in your trading methodology if you know that your exact rules have been tried and tested and worked very well in the past. You won't have to look at your stocks every day and you won't have to make decisions under pressure.

Using the building blocks that have been described earlier, let's create a complete strategy with exact rules for how to trade. Once you have firm rules, you can either see it as a check list which you manually work through at specified intervals, or you can go a step further and automate the entire process.

Having these rules, you can of course also construct a proper simulation and back test the concept. This will give you added confidence as well as giving you reasonable expectations of performance. It's important to understand what kind of return profile you can expect, both in good and bad times.

In the strategy I'll describe in this chapter, I will use some exact parameters. I will use a certain number of days to calculate volatility and momentum, as well as other factors. Don't focus overly much on the numbers I've chosen. A solid trading strategy isn't very sensitive to these kinds of numbers. The numbers I'll use here make sense, but so do other numbers. The concept is key. Don't lose track of that. If this strategy only worked with these exact parameters, it would be useless. I'll offer these settings as a starting point, but I encourage you to experiment with different values.

The Exact Trading Rules

Yes, I used the heading above to help those who skipped ahead, searching for just the trading rules. This is where I'll list the rules.

- Trade only on Wednesdays.

What we're dealing with here is a long term method of beating the stock market. Part of such a strategy is to avoid acting too fast. To reduce both workload and trading frequency, we'll only check for trade signals once per week. It doesn't matter if a stock plunges 20% in a day, unless that's the day we're supposed to trade we don't do a thing. Note that this doesn't mean that we work with weekly data. All calculations are done on daily data. We just don't trade unless it's a Wednesday. Why Wednesday of all days? Because Wednesdays happen to have a 20% probability of being the best possible weekday to trade. Yes, it's absolutely arbitrary. Pick a day. It doesn't matter.

- Rank all stocks based on volatility adjusted momentum.

Rank all stocks in the S&P 500 Index based on momentum. We'll use annualized exponential regression slope, calculated on the past 90 days, and then multiply it with the coefficient of determination (R^2) for the same period. This gives us a volatility adjusted momentum measurement.

Remember that if a stock is trading below its 100 day moving average or has a recent gap in excess of 15%, it's disqualified.

- Calculate position sizes, based on 10 basis points.

Calculate position size, using a simple ATR based formula, targeting a daily move of 10 basis points. The formula to calculate number of shares is $AccountValue * 0.001 / ATR_{20}$.

- Check index filter.

You're only allowed to open new positions if the S&P 500 Index is above its 200 day moving average. If it's below, no new buys are allowed.

- Construct the initial portfolio.

Start from the top of your ranking list. If the first stock is not disqualified by being below its 100 day moving average or having a 15%+ gap, then buy it and move to the next. Buy from the top until you run out of cash.

- Rebalance portfolio every Wednesday.

Once a week we check if any stock needs to be sold. If a stock is no longer in the top 20% of the S&P 500 stocks, based on the ranking, we sell it. If it's trading below its 100 day moving average, we sell it. If it had a gap over 15%, we sell it. If it left the index, we sell it.

If we have available cash, we look for stocks to buy. If any stock is being sold, there is of course cash available. Buying replacement stocks follow the same logic as above. Only buy if the index is in a positive trend. Buy from the top of the ranking list, if it's in the top 20%, has positive trend and doesn't have a large gap. As long as the index is in a positive trend, we just buy new stocks from the top of the list until we run out of cash again.

- Rebalance positions every second Wednesday.

Twice per month we reset position sizes. As explained earlier, a long term strategy needs to incorporate position size rebalancing to avoid ending up with a completely random risk. Go over each position in your portfolio, compare your current position size with the target size. Calculate target size based on the exact same formula as you used to begin with, but of course with the updated portfolio size and ATR.

If the difference is minor, there's no need to rebalance just for the sake of it. This procedure is here to make sure position risk doesn't spin out of control. If there's any significant deviation, reset position size to target size.

Well, that's about it. Wait, let's look at that again.

Ok, you only need to check the markets once a week. I picked Wednesday completely at random, so please don't send me emails about whether some moon cycle pattern makes Wednesday the best day. Pick whatever day you prefer.

So we only look at the market on Wednesdays. Every week we check first if we should sell any positions. If a position no longer qualifies, it's sold. Then if we have available cash, and the index is in a positive trend, we buy stocks. Start at the top of the rankings list and buy until you have no more cash.

Every second Wednesday, we have a have an additional task. Compare position target sizes with actual sizes, and rebalance as needed.

That's an easy check list, isn't it? Sure, let's make it even easier. Just print the flow chart in Figure 10-1.

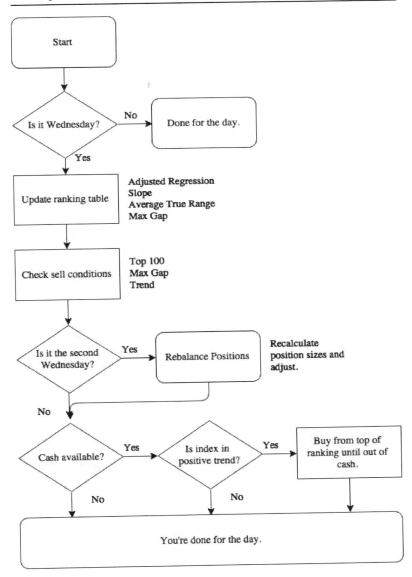

Figure 10-1 Trading Rules Flow Chart

11

Trading the Strategy

Perhaps the whole momentum strategy seems a bit theoretical at this point. It might help if we take a look at the practical side and see how you would actually implement it. We'll also review some charts to see where stocks would have been bought and sold.

The Initial Portfolio

The day you launch your strategy, you jump right into the deep end of the pool. No gradual buying. Given that the market regime is positive, that is if the index is trading above its 200 day moving average, we just buy stocks until we're out of cash.

Obviously the first task here is to make sure that the S&P 500 is trading above the moving average. This part is easy. Any charting software can do that for you, and you could even do it in Excel if you want by just comparing the average of the last 200 index prices to the current one. If the index is below the moving average, we don't buy a thing. Just sit tight and wait for it to come back up into positive territory.

Now you need to calculate the relevant analytics mentioned in previous chapters and make a neat little ranking table. Doing this manually for one stock is easy enough, but we need it for hundreds of stocks. Some readers may think this is a piece of cake to get done while others have no idea where to start.

What you want to come up with is something like Table 11-1. Naturally the actual data in this table is not up to date by the time you read this. This table forms the core of the entire strategy. It's a very important table, so let's go over the crucial columns.

The slope column is probably the most important one. That's what the table is sorted on and that's what governs the priority of our purchases.

The slope column shows the volatility adjusted slope, as explained in chapter 7. Briefly, this number is simply a measurement of the momentum a stock is showing, adjusted for volatility. The higher the number, the better the risk adjusted performance has been. We want to buy a portfolio of as high numbers as possible.

Even if a stock has a very high rank, it could still be disqualified. There are two more columns we need to check before knowing if we're allowed to buy a stock or not. The Trend column tells you whether or not the stock is above its 100 day moving average. If it's not, we're not buying it. It's unusual for a stock to have a very high ranking and still be below this average, but it can happen. This is a bit of a failsafe to avoid some weird situations.

Then there's the maximum gap. We're not looking for stocks that suddenly made a 40% jump on a takeover rumor. We're looking for orderly bull markets, stocks moving up in a controlled fashion. Some gaps have to be accepted but we don't want to jump into these odd situations where a single, huge gap caused the stock to jump to the top of the ranking table. The maximum gap we'll allow for the past 90 days is 15%. That means that the top entry in this particular table, Hospira, is disqualified. It had a recent gap of 26%, so we're not considering that stock.

Next we've got the ATR, or Average True Range. This number tells us how much a stock tends to move up or down on an average day, in dollars. This we'll use for position sizing. Remember that we're aiming for a risk parity portfolio, where every stock has an equal theoretical chance to impact the overall portfolio.

The Target% column is a new one. All the other data here has been explained before, but not this one. At least not directly. This is a useful thing to have in a ranking table and it tells you how large weight of a particular stock you should target. It's easily calculated based on the ATR column.

Since Hospira has too large of a gap, we're skipping that one. Let's buy Mallinckrodt to begin with and let's calculate how many shares we'll need to buy.

We're using a risk factor of 10 basis points here. That means that we'd like each stock to have a daily average profit or loss impact on our portfolio of 0.1%. Let's say we're starting out with an account worth $100,000. In this case, we want each stock to move by about $100 per day on average.

Mallinckrodt has an ATR of 3.69 according to the table, meaning that the share price has shown average daily moves of that amount in the recent past. Since each stock moves around $3.69 per day and we want an impact of $100, we'd have to buy 27 shares. 27 multiplied by 3.69 is close enough to 100.

The share price at the time this table was made was about $126. Multiply 126 by our 27 shares, and we'll come with an exposure of $3,414. If you divide that by your account value of $100,000, you'll find that you've got a weight for this position of 3.4%.

Now move onto the next stock, and keep buying until you're out of cash.

Table 11-1 Ranking Table

Rank	Name	Slope	ATR	Max Gap	Trend	Target%	Ticker
1	Hospira Inc	279.2	0.64	26.0	1	13.7	HSP
2	Mallinckrodt Plc	198.9	3.69	6.9	1	3.4	MNK
3	Biogen Idec Inc	168.7	13.44	9.4	1	3.4	BIIB
4	Avago Technologies	164.1	3.48	11.2	1	3.9	AVGO
5	Urban Outfitters Inc	157.9	1.20	9.2	1	3.9	URBN
6	Boston Scientific	149.2	0.48	11.1	1	3.7	BSX
7	Electronic Arts Inc	145.5	1.36	11.5	1	4.3	EA
8	Kohl's Corp	134.7	1.28	5.9	1	5.9	KSS
9	Kroger Co	129.0	1.27	6.3	1	6.1	KR
10	Vulcan Materials Co	123.1	1.51	4.5	1	5.7	VMC
11	Constellation Brands	110.5	2.04	4.3	1	5.8	STZ
12	Netflix Inc	105.3	11.7	15.0	1	3.7	NFLX
13	Harman Int	97.8	3.69	19.2	1	3.7	HAR
14	Newmont Mining	94.8	0.81	8.6	1	2.8	NEM
15	Monster Beverage	94.5	3.77	11.5	1	3.7	MNST

16	Dollar Tree Inc	93.8	1.42	4.9	1	5.8 DLTR
17	Laboratory Corp	93.2	2.17	3.3	1	5.9 LH
18	Mohawk Industries	90.9	3.77	6.2	1	4.8 MHK
20	Cigna Corp	84.7	2.36	4.9	1	5.5 CI
21	International Flavors	80.6	2.16	6.8	1	5.6 IFF
23	Aetna Inc	78.7	1.87	3.3	1	5.8 AET
24	Lowe's Companies	78.6	1.31	6.0	1	5.8 LOW
25	UnitedHealth Group	78.6	2.19	4.6	1	5.4 UNH
26	Humana Inc	78.4	3.77	5.1	1	4.8 HUM
27	Starbucks Corp	78.1	1.70	6.0	1	5.7 SBUX
28	Valero Energy Corp	77.3	1.66	5.3	1	3.7 VLO
29	Home Depot Inc	75.4	2.01	4.1	1	5.8 HD
30	Boeing Co	74.6	2.56	5.6	1	5.9 BA
31	Sherwin-Williams	73.8	4.24	3.0	1	6.8 SHW
32	AmerisourceBergen	71.7	1.80	3.6	1	6.3 ABC
33	Equifax Inc	71.6	1.06	7.8	1	8.7 EFX
34	Coach Inc	70.9	0.88	6.3	1	4.8 COH
35	L Brands Inc	70.7	1.68	5.1	1	5.6 LB
36	Ross Stores Inc	70.6	2.01	6.6	1	5.3 ROST
37	General Motors Co	70.5	0.74	5.1	1	5.1 GM
37	General Motors Co	70.5	0.74	5.1	1	5.1 GM
38	Cognizant Tech	69.8	1.06	4.8	1	5.9 CTSH
40	Walt Disney Co	69.0	1.74	7.2	1	6.2 DIS

The trade chart shown in Figure 11-1 demonstrates how a trade is done. The various lines you see in that figure are not traditional technical indicators, but rather specific items for this momentum model that I find useful to visualize.

At the top of this figure, you'll see the actual price chart of the stock, Urban Outfitters. A 100 day moving average line is drawn on top of it, to show that the stock is currently in a positive trend. The second chart pane, just below, shows the S&P 500 index with a 200 day moving average. This clearly displays that the index at this point in time is also positive, trading above the moving average.

Next the risk adjusted momentum slope is shown. This analytic is explained in chapter 7. Then there's the ATR, showing how the volatility of the stock is changing all the time, necessitating us to continuously change our position size in order to keep risks in line.

The momentum rank in the next pane tells us where this stock ranks, compared to all other stocks in the index. So if you take the risk adjusted momentum slope of all stocks in the index and sort them on this as we did in Table 11-1, this indicator tells us where in that table this particular stock shows up. A low number means a strong risk adjusted momentum compared to everyone else.

The index member indicator is either 1 if the stock is currently a part of the index in question, or 0 if it's not. Taking historical index composition into account is absolutely critical. You need to have a formal constraint to which stocks are part of your investment universe and which are not. The easiest way to make a great looking simulation with utterly useless results is to assume that you trade the current index members ten years ago.

If a stock isn't part of the index, we don't trade it. If it leaves the index, we sell it.

Finally the last chart pane shows how large the maximum gap was in the stock, in the past 90 days. As long as this is below 15%, we're all good.

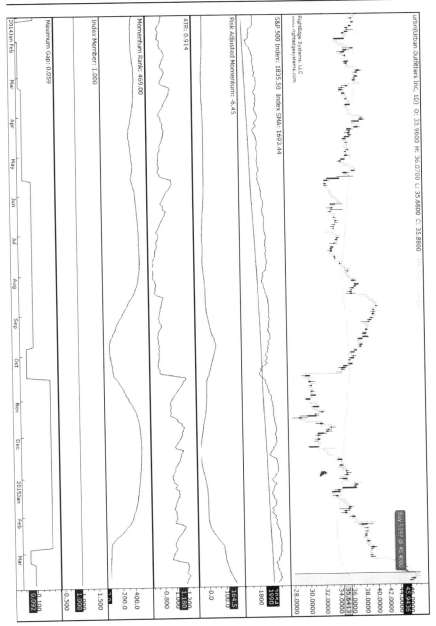

Figure 11-1 Trade chart: Buying Urban Outfitters

As can be seen here, we bought Urban Outfitters in March of 2015, after it had a strong run up. Note how the risk adjusted momentum series started moving up, causing the stock to rise in the ranking list. At the start of the year, this stock had a rank of over 400, meaning it was a terrible performer. Then it started taking off, quickly climbing up the table until it was finally bought.

That's how you construct your initial portfolio. Just buy from the top, as long as the stock passes the filters. But the work is not over yet. Now you have to do the regular rebalancing tasks to ensure that you've always got the portfolio composition we're targeting.

Position Rebalancing

Twice per month, every second week, we rebalance position sizes. It's a matter of preference if you want to do this a bit more often or a bit farther apart. Do it with higher frequency and you'll have a more accurate risk, but at the same time incur higher trading costs. Every second week is a good compromise.

The purpose of the position rebalancing is to keep the risks in line. The volatility of stocks changes over time and since we need a risk parity portfolio, we need to keep adjusting the trade size to match our target risk per stock.

The idea of one buy and one sell per position is outdated. That's not how you manage a portfolio. All these rebalance trades can make a trade chart look quite confusing, but it really does make a lot of sense.

The first thing to do is to make an updated ranking table, just like Table 11-1. This will tell you the target weights of each stock. Now you need to compare with your actual weights and make the necessary adjustment.

In Figure 11-2 you see the trades done for the momentum strategy in Java during 1999 and 2000. The initial purchase was done in September 1999 where 387 shares were bought for this portfolio. As the volatility kept moving up, seen in the ATR pane, a small amount of shares were sold at each position rebalance. These sales have nothing to do with market view. We're not selling because we think that the share price might go down and we're not selling to take home profits or anything like that. We're selling because we want to maintain our initial risk. If we don't sell some shares, we would end up with a higher risk than we had intended.

It's important to understand this point. If we do nothing, our position changes. We need to act to maintain our intended position. This could mean buying shares or selling shares but it has no bearing on market views.

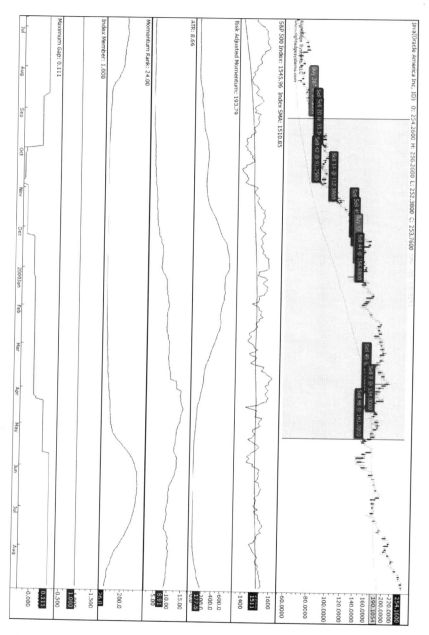

Figure 11-2 Trade Chart: Oracle

Portfolio Rebalance

The portfolio rebalance is done every week. The point with this exercise is to exit positions that no longer fulfill our criteria and to buy new ones. Of course, if the index is not above its long term moving average, we're not replacing the stocks and thereby scaling down our overall portfolio risk.

Again, we have to start by making an updated ranking table. Start by going over the stocks that you currently own. If any stock shows a negative trend, as in trading below its 100 day moving average, sell it. If any stock had a gap in excess of 15%, sell it.

If the stock is no longer part of the top 100 stocks in the index, sell it. If we're looking at the stocks in the S&P 500, that means that the rank needs to be better than 100. Make the ranking table, sort on the volatility adjusted momentum slope and check where the stock ends up. Higher number than 100, and out the door it goes.

Once you're done selling the stocks that no longer belong in the portfolio, you're ready to buy new ones. And you already know how to do that, don't you? The same way as we picked the initial stocks. Start at the top of the ranking table. Given that we don't already own the stock and that it fulfills the criteria, we buy the highest ranking stocks until we're out of cash again.

Unless of course, and this is important, unless the index is below the moving average. If it's below, we simply keep the cash and don't buy any new stocks. The result will be a slow and gradual scaling out of the stock market during a bear phase.

Once the index again pokes its head above the moving average, we instantly rebuy a fully loaded portfolio. This is done the exact same way as with the initial portfolio. Just buy from the top of the list until you're out of cash.

The Gilead trade chart in Figure 11-3 shows how we first bought the stock in May of 2005, changed the size a bit during the summer due to changing volatility and finally sold it again in August. The ranking worsened during the late summer and resulted in selling the whole position.

Later that year, in December, the stock again showed a very high momentum ranking. The stock was rebought and held for another few months.

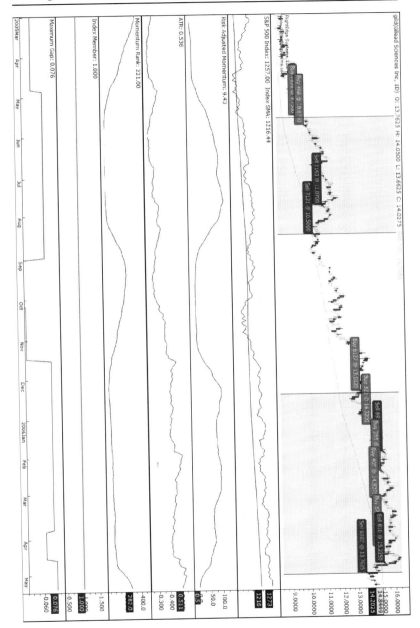

Figure 11-3 Trade chart: Gilead

12
Momentum Strategy
Performance

We now have a complete equity momentum strategy. So far we've looked at the various components of the strategy but we haven't seen the actual results yet. Before looking at the historical performance of this approach, stop and consider what is realistic to expect.

This is not a strategy where you can expect a steady 10% a year. Very few strategies are. It's not a strategy where you can expect every year to be positive. And it's certainly not a strategy that should be expected to be uncorrelated to the equity markets. We are after all buying stocks. Strategies based on buying stocks tend to look very similar in the long run. Some are better, some are worse, but they will be correlated.

What we can hope for is to show strong performance in bull markets and to lose less than the index in bear markets. If we do that, we'll have very attractive returns in the long run.

The first question is of course, whether or not we're outperforming the market. If we're making money but not beating the index, then there's really no point in all this effort. A quick glance at Figure 12-1 should set your mind at ease in that regard.

As this is a long term chart with large percentage moves, a standard price chart can be a bit misleading however and easily gives an exaggerated performance impression. Therefore, a log version of the same performance chart can be found in Figure 12-2.

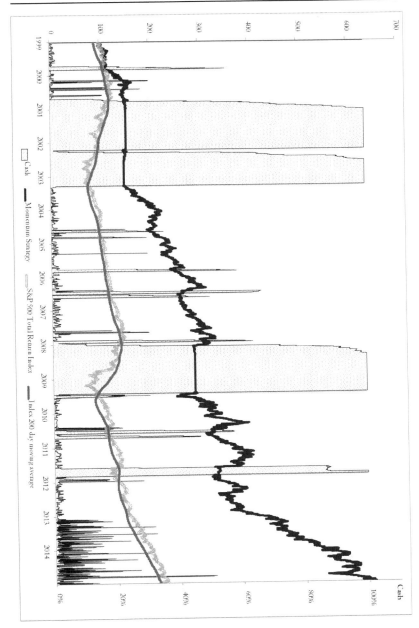

Figure 12-1 Strategy Long Term Performance

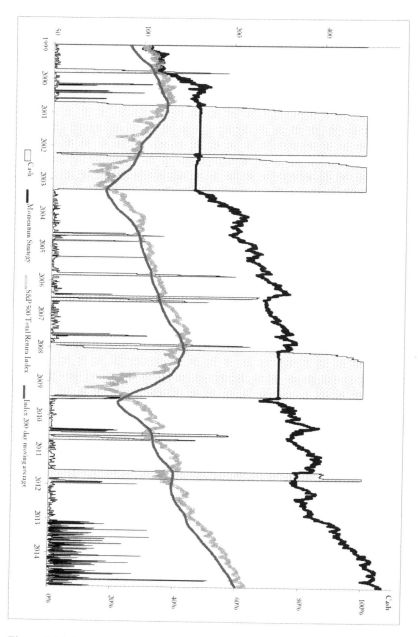

Figure 12-2 Strategy Long Term Performance, Log Scale

We are outperforming. We're even outperforming quite a bit. As you can see visually, there are two different types of outperformance. There are periods where we are showing strong outperformance in bull markets. But in terms of relative performance, there's an even larger effect from simply not being invested in stocks when the markets are falling.

And how well did we do in the end?

Table 12-1 Momentum Strategy Results

	Momentum Strategy	S&P 500 Total Return
Annualized Return	12.3%	5.2%
Maximum Drawdown	-24%	-55%

As Table 12-1 shows, the momentum strategy yielded over 12% annualized over this 16 year period. You don't think 12% per year is good enough? Think again. The equity markets as a whole accomplished only 5% per year for this period. Had you been invested in mutual funds, you would have gotten even lower returns.

Put the returns into proper context. Warren Buffett has achieved legendary status by showing an amazing 22% annualized return over the past 40 years. Aiming for such high number over prolonged periods is unrealistic. There are extremely few people in the world who have achieved that and most of them are now billionaires.

If you can compound in the low double digits over time, you're beating almost everyone out there. The stock markets as a whole only give 5-6% per year on average over long term periods.

Most importantly though, we achieved our 12% at less than half the drawdowns of the index. Drawdown refers to the maximum loss we've seen during the time period. The S&P 500 total return index saw a maximum loss of 55%. Over half the capital was gone at one point. Our momentum approach on the other hand only had a maximum loss of 24%.

Another way to look at those numbers is that the index lost 11 years' worth of performance while the momentum strategy only lost 2. Consider if you enter at the worst possible time, and how long it would take for you to recover your losses.

Table 12-2 will show you the month by month performance of our momentum strategy. It's hard to get a feeling for a strategy just by looking at a monthly return table, so in the next chapter we'll go into all the details and look at how the strategy performed each year.

Table 12-2 Core Equity Momentum Strategy Performance

	Jan (%)	Feb (%)	Mar (%)	Apr (%)	May (%)	Jun (%)	Jul (%)	Aug (%)	Sep (%)	Oct (%)	Nov (%)	Dec (%)	Year (%)
1999	6.3	-5.1	9.8	1.6	-3.1	3.5	-2.5	2.1	-2.6	3.5	7.9	15.2	**41.0**
2000	-5.1	14.0	3.8	-1.6	-1.9	-3.4	-3.4	5.3	4.3	-2.1	0.1	0.6	**9.6**
2001	-0.7	0.0	0.0	0.0	0.0	0.0	0.0	0.0	0.0	0.0	0.0	0.0	**-0.7**
2002	0.0	0.0	-1.1	0.3	-0.2	-0.7	-1.3	0.0	0.0	0.0	0.0	0.0	**-3.0**
2003	0.0	0.0	0.0	2.1	7.4	0.5	5.5	6.3	-3.2	13.3	3.0	1.6	**41.8**
2004	2.8	0.2	-3.5	-3.4	1.0	4.3	-3.3	-2.0	4.9	3.7	7.1	1.9	**13.7**
2005	-3.6	5.9	-2.3	-4.4	2.3	4.8	3.9	0.5	4.5	-6.8	3.4	1.6	**9.3**
2006	10.1	-1.9	4.2	0.9	-6.5	-4.4	-2.4	0.6	-0.6	1.7	1.2	0.4	**2.4**
2007	4.4	-0.3	1.6	3.8	3.7	-1.7	0.9	-0.5	5.3	3.6	-5.7	1.5	**17.3**
2008	-8.6	-0.2	-0.2	0.4	0.0	0.0	0.0	0.0	0.0	0.0	0.0	0.0	**-8.5**
2009	0.0	0.0	0.0	0.0	0.0	-7.3	9.0	4.7	2.7	-5.7	6.5	4.5	**14.0**
2010	-5.8	6.0	9.9	4.2	-8.2	-7.2	0.1	-2.3	4.6	4.6	1.3	5.7	**11.7**
2011	0.5	7.5	1.1	-0.9	-3.1	-2.7	-1.5	-8.8	-1.0	-1.3	1.7	-0.5	**-9.3**
2012	5.6	6.0	3.3	-2.8	-7.2	2.8	-0.4	1.1	3.3	-0.2	3.0	3.6	**18.9**
2013	10.0	0.3	7.9	-4.1	1.6	0.1	5.1	-2.2	4.0	5.8	2.6	2.1	**37.5**
2014	1.9	5.9	-1.0	-1.7	2.4	5.3	-4.4	4.3	-2.0	-1.1	6.9	1.3	**18.4**

13
Year by Year Review

When writing my first book, *Following the Trend*, which is about trend following futures strategies, I struggled with how to best convey what it's really like to be a professional asset manager. Just showing some simulation statistics and long term performance graphs really doesn't show the day to day struggle. Quite often, a strategy can look great when you've got a multi-decade perspective but it may still be very tough or even impossible to execute in reality. It's only when the proverbial rubber meets the road that we'll really find out what works and what doesn't.

My solution in that book was to write a monster chapter where I explained, year by year, how that trading strategy had performed in the past. It wasn't my intention for that chapter to end up dominating the book, but that's what happened. In the end, that chapter took up almost a third of the book. This made me wonder if I should really include it. Personally, I found it to be by far the most important part of that book. It's the chapter that explains the tough parts. What it's really like to sit in a 25% drawdown, having clients pulling out money, seeing revenues plummeting and wondering if the business is over. These situations will happen. Only if you have full understanding of your trading method and how it behaves in difficult situations, only then can you have the confidence to continue though the tough periods.

My worry was that the year-by-year chapter would be seen by readers as a page-filler. As it turned out, I had underestimated my readers. The number one most common feedback that I got on that book was how much people learnt from that particular chapter. How this was the chapter that gave a sense of reality and explained the things that are usually glossed over.

As this was a very popular part of my previous book, I will attempt to do the same here.

1999

It's January 1999. The internet is at the center of the universe. Electronic mails provide a whole new way to avoid human contact. Profits are for losers. The Information Gold Rush is on and there's no time for old accounting concepts.

In the madness that was the late 90's, we go live with our brand new momentum strategy. It's a great time to launch such a strategy. That is, at least in terms of raising money for it. Having had an absolutely amazing decade, everyone's got plenty of money. The past decade has also taught us that all you have to do is to buy things that move. Don't worry about revenue, profit, even cash flow. This is a very special time. The inmates have clearly taken over the asylum and there's nothing to be gained by wearing a guard's uniform. If there was ever a time where no one would question an equity momentum strategy, this was it.

If you weren't actively trading during this time, it would be very hard to understand the extent of the madness. Any stock even remotely associated with the magical words "IT", "Internet", "World Wide Web" and "Dot Com" had sky high valuations, absolutely regardless of whether or not they made any money. Even regardless of whether they had any realistic prospects of ever making any money.

The market place at the time clearly didn't understand anything about any of these companies. That's clear now, but was far from clear at the time. The rationale for buying shares in extremely overvalued, loss making companies was that probably someone else can see the value, and if I don't buy it someone else will. Perhaps there will be a takeover soon by someone who can see the massive profit potential, which surely must be there somewhere.

The fact that we were all buying tulip bulbs didn't really occur to many people. After the fact however, most people's memories would beg to differ. This is actually a very good year for us to start our journey. First, because it's a very likely year for someone to start such a strategy. It made perfect sense in those market conditions. The second good reason for starting this year is to see how it handled the transition period. The hangover from the 90's party was quite severe and lingered for a long time. What better test for our momentum strategy than to start during the party times and see how it handles the inevitable crash?

We start our portfolio just after the 1998 New Year's party. We run the calculations, crunch the numbers, rank the stocks and build our portfolio. Just like it's been explained in the previous chapters. The index gives us a green light, with prices far above the 200 day moving average. While there was a brief dip below it during the exciting 1998, which had Russia along with a few Nobel Prize winners playing lead roles, the market quickly recovered.

The initial portfolio was constructed by making a table that ranks all stocks by volatility adjusted momentum, calculates the target weights and all other analytics described in earlier chapters, and then just buying from the top of that list until there's no more cash. Table 13-1 shows what this resulted in.

Table 13-1 Initial Portfolio 1999

Name	Weight	Sector
Applied Biosystems Inc	3.7%	Health Care
Adobe Systems Inc	2.0%	Information Technology
Autodesk Inc	2.2%	Information Technology
Applied Materials Inc	1.9%	Information Technology
Avon Products Inc	2.5%	Consumer Staples
Brunswick Corp	3.2%	Consumer Discretionary
Bank of New York Mellon Corp	3.3%	Financials
Bausch & Lomb Inc	3.9%	Consumer Staples
Coca-Cola Enterprises Inc	2.5%	Consumer Staples
3Com Corp	2.0%	Information Technology
EMC Corp	2.8%	Information Technology
FedEx Corp	3.1%	Industrials
Federal Home Loan Mortgage Corp	3.7%	Financials
Corning Inc	3.8%	Information Technology
Gap Inc	2.3%	Consumer Discretionary
IBM	4.5%	Information Technology
Intel Corp	2.9%	Information Technology

Oracle America Inc	2.6% Information Technology
JPMorgan Chase & Co	2.9% Financials
Kimberly-Clark Corp	4.4% Consumer Staples
LSI Corp	1.8% Information Technology
Mallinckrodt LLC	3.8% Health Care
Motorola Solutions Inc	3.4% Information Technology
Micron Technology Inc	2.0% Information Technology
Novell Inc	2.8% Information Technology
Oracle Corp	1.8% Information Technology
Charles Schwab Corp	1.8% Financials
SLM Corp	3.4% Financials
Solectron Corp	2.7% Industrials
Staples Inc	2.2% Consumer Discretionary
State Street Corp	4.0% Financials
Tektronix Inc	2.7% Information Technology
Texas Instruments Inc	2.8% Information Technology
United Technologies Corp	3.8% Industrials

It should come as no surprise that our initial portfolio is heavily overweight in tech stocks. This was the sector that moved the most at the time and many of the top ranked stocks are therefore from that group. There are no constraints as to sector allocation here. We just buy from the top of the list, no matter what sector they might be.

We ended up with 42% IT stocks, 19% financials, 13% staples, 10% industrials, 8% discretionary and 8% health care. No stocks were bought in utilities, telecom, energy or materials stocks. That's quite a different profile from the index.

There are quite a few stocks in the portfolio. 34 stocks is more than what's usually needed for diversification. The reason that there are so many stocks is that we're dealing with very volatile markets here. Most of these stocks are hyper volatile tech stocks. Now remember how the position sizing was done. The details of this were explained in chapter 8. The more volatile a stock is the smaller amount of cash we'll allocate to it.

This is a common approach among professional asset managers, to ensure that you have approximately equal risk in each investment, instead of letting volatility run wild.

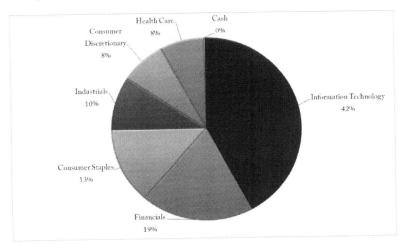

Figure 13-1 Initial Sector Allocation, 1999

The year started quite slow. For the first quarter of the year, the trading results were very close to what the index produced. Even after a brief period of outperformance in April, the results continued to hug the index. Since the index mostly went up, that wasn't necessarily a problem. Outperforming is nice, but most of us care more about the absolute return. While it was a positive period, up until September it was a surprisingly boring year. Compared to the run-away markets we had all gotten used to in the 90's, it just didn't feel sufficient to only have a 20% gain at the end of the third quarter. A long term bull market can spoil anyone.

In September however the market started worrying many people. There had been several months without making a new all-time high, and that was quite unusual. The S&P 500 Index was creeping slowly closer and closer to its 200 day moving average, and then in September it finally plunged through it.

Remember that this cross itself doesn't trigger anything. However, when the index is below the moving average, we're not allowed to buy any new positions. As stocks were sold in the regular portfolio rebalancing, they were not replaced. That left us with a slowly increasing pile of cash in late 1999.

You can see in Figure 13-2 how the cash started building up in October, as the index dipped under the water line. The cash percentage is shown as a filled area, using the right y-axis. There's usually a little bit of cash laying around. If there's not enough liquidity available to buy a whole position, we just leave it in cash. See it as a rounding error if you will.

Note in the figure how the index moves below the long term moving average in September and how the cash slowly starts building up after that. As positions are exited during the regular rebalancing task, they are not being replaced as long as the index remains under the moving average. This is a key feature of this strategy, and it means that we will automatically scale out of potential bear markets.

In late October, we're holding about half of the portfolio in plain cash and the performance on the year is about equal to the benchmark. So far, that doesn't look too impressive. Had you launched this strategy at the start of 1999, you'd probably be quite tempted to call it quits, or at least change the rules. For the better part of a year, you've been doing all this work and there's nothing to show for it. Sure, we have a profit but so do passive index investors.

But then, just before the start of November, something is happening. The first thing that happens is that the index bobs up over the moving average again, giving us a green signal to start buying. That's usually quite a scary point. We had just closed out most positions, the markets are looking increasingly tired, there's a potential bear market looming, and we're now buying a full portfolio of stocks.

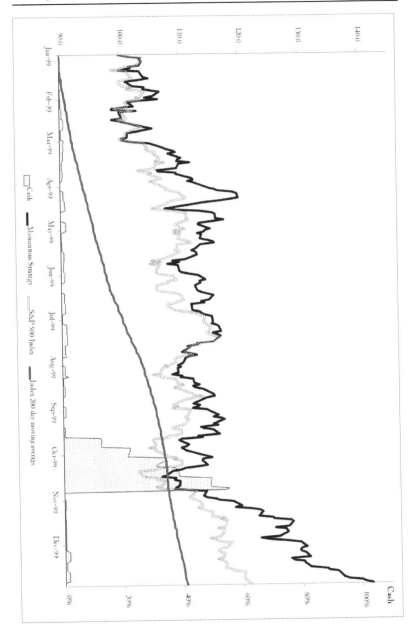

Figure 13-2 Performance, 1999

Yep, that's what we're doing. We make the ranking list again and start buying from the top until we're all out of cash. As the trend light turned green on the last day of October, we bought 19 new positions from the top of the list.

This newly reconstructed portfolio then suddenly took off in a big way. The index recovered well, but our stocks did very much better. As the index ended the year at +20%, this incredible end of year rally brought our portfolio all the way up to over 40% on the year. Now those doubts that likely lingered around October should finally be put to rest.

There were multiple stocks responsible for the dramatic boost in performance that we saw by the end of the year. One of these was Entrasys Networks, illustrated in Figure 13-3. This is a perfect example of what you want to see. The share price had been advancing for a few months and it was ranked highly among the peers. The position on the ranking list is shown in the bottom pane. A lower number means a better momentum ranking. In the rebalancing on the 29th of October, all systems are go and we buy this stock at about $80.50. This stock waits for no man and takes off right away. The price kept accelerating all the way up and when it was reaching around the $200 levels, it made a large gap up before consolidating.

Remember how we have that gap filter in the strategy? In the rebalancing process, any stock which had a recent gap of over 15% is automatically disqualified, even if the gap was in our favor. In this case, it means that we sell this stock in the next rebalance. As it turns out, that was a perfect place to sell. If only every trade was this great.

Table 13-2 Results 1999

	Momentum Strategy	S&P 500 Total Return Index
Return 1999	41.0%	21.1%
Max Drawdown 1999	-11.1%	-11.8%

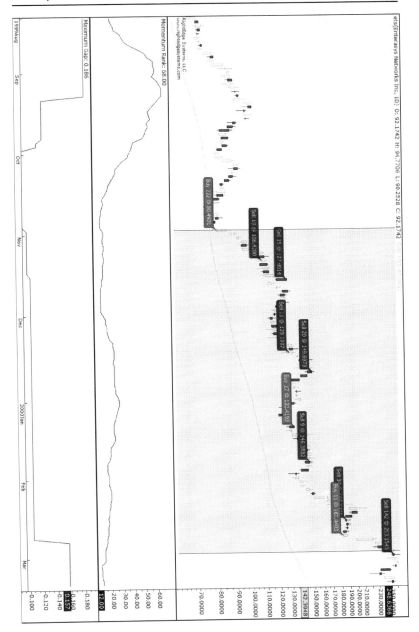

Figure 13-3 Enterasys Networks

2000

When we enter into 2000 there are no real signs of a market reversal. We had a very long lasting bull market behind us and there was no reason to think that it might end soon. The indexes had slowed a bit, and we were getting closer to the 200 day moving average. That has happened before though and in itself that wasn't too worrying.

So we enter into the new millennium fully loaded. The portfolio is still heavily overweight in IT stocks, with half of the value placed in this sector. The remaining portfolio is spread over multiple sectors, with the largest weight being in health care. With the hindsight knowledge of what happened to IT stocks in the new decade, this initial portfolio allocation seems rather ominous. Is this the year that we see a crash in our portfolio?

Table 13-3 Initial Portfolio, 2000

Name	Weight	Sector
Apple Inc	1.8%	Information Technology
Applied Biosystems Inc	4.4%	Health Care
Adobe Systems Inc	1.6%	Information Technology
Analog Devices Inc	2.4%	Information Technology
Applied Materials Inc	2.1%	Information Technology
Amgen Inc	3.1%	Health Care
BMC Software Inc	1.8%	Information Technology
Comverse Technology Inc	2.8%	Information Technology
3Com Corp	1.3%	Information Technology
Cisco Systems Inc	2.9%	Information Technology
Dow Jones & Company Inc	3.7%	Financials
EMC Corp	2.8%	Information Technology
Enterasys Networks Inc	1.6%	Information Technology
General Instrument Corp	2.5%	Information Technology
Corning Inc	2.6%	Information Technology
Home Depot Inc	4.1%	Consumer Discretionary
Oracle America Inc	2.3%	Information Technology
KLA-Tencor Corp	2.0%	Information Technology

Lehman Brothers Holdings Inc	3.0%	Financials
Molex Inc	2.4%	Information Technology
Morgan Stanley	3.6%	Financials
Motorola Solutions Inc	2.5%	Information Technology
Nortel Networks Corp	2.3%	Information Technology
Nextel Communications Inc	1.6%	Telecommunication Services
Oracle Corp	2.1%	Information Technology
Paychex Inc	1.9%	Information Technology
Procter & Gamble Co	3.9%	Consumer Staples
PerkinElmer Inc	3.0%	Health Care
Qualcomm Inc	2.5%	Information Technology
Sprint Corp	3.2%	Telecommunication Services
Solectron Corp	2.8%	Industrials
Sysco Corp	3.8%	Consumer Staples
Tenet Healthcare Corp	2.6%	Health Care
Time Warner Inc	1.6%	Consumer Discretionary
Texas Instruments Inc	2.1%	Information Technology
Warner-Lambert Company LLC	3.1%	Health Care
Wal-Mart Stores Inc	3.1%	Consumer Staples
Xilinx Inc	1.6%	Information Technology

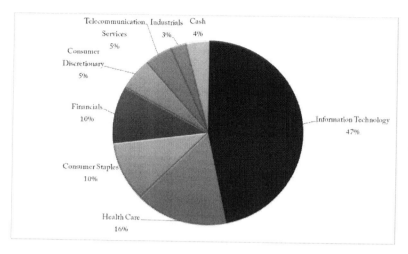

Figure 13-4 Initial Sector Allocation, 2000

The year started with some quite worrying volatility. In the first three trading days of the new year, the S&P 500 Index lost almost 7%, and our momentum strategy lost 8%. That's quite dramatic and if you had launched the strategy this year instead of last year, you'd be forgiven for throwing in the towel after the first week. Don't underestimate the impact of these drawdowns. It's very easy to look back at a 15 year simulated equity curve and say that these little blips don't really matter. It's a whole different thing when you're trading real money and see real losses. When you're looking at those long term simulations, you know how the story will turn out. When you're in the middle of such a situation in reality, you have no idea. For all you know, you might see another 8% loss before the week is over. Perhaps a worse week after that. And the problem is that these situations are far more common than one might think.

This is a why this very chapter is included in this book. The point is to demonstrate these problems and prepare you for what might happen. After those first three days, having lost 8%, anyone would be very tempted to override the rules or even shut the whole thing down.

In this case it turned out pretty ok though. The portfolio volatility in the first couple of weeks was enormous, but two weeks into the year, we were already back to the zero line. The chaotic market conditions continued for a few more weeks and we saw big swings in the bottom line. In February however, the momentum strategy really took off.

Multiple stocks started running wild on the upside, accumulating profits rapidly. By the end of the first quarter we saw portfolio returns of over 15% on the year. Suddenly no one can even remember that we started the year at -8%. When you see such spectacular returns so early in the year, it's only natural that you start calculating your year-end result, assuming you'll get the same performance for the whole year. 15% in three month would mean 75% in a year. Yes, that's not a typo. It's not 45%, but rather 75%, as in 1.15^4. This is a type of calculation that's very tempting to make, but it can also be quite dangerous. It's highly unlikely that such a scenario will play out and it will only serve to make your expectations very unrealistic.

As seen in Figure 13-5, the stellar results this year didn't last very long. As the IT stocks started falling and the markets suddenly started worrying about outdated concepts such as 'profits', our portfolio saw rapid declines. Already in April, we're once again introduced to the once distant zero line.

Note how the cash starts building up from March on. By May we had liquidated over 30% of the portfolio. Stocks started falling across the board, and suddenly there were not many possible candidate stocks. Most stocks found themselves trading below their 100 day moving average and were therefore disqualified from being bought. Many also made daily moves in excess of 15%, also ruling themselves out from the list of candidates.

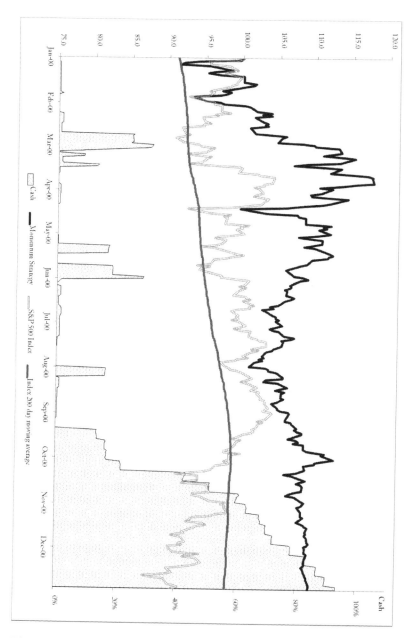

Figure 13-5 Year Performance, 2000

After that, most of the year went sideways. We started building up a portfolio again during the summer as the index came up a little bit and there were more available stocks to buy. This time however, the sector allocation looked very different. In the beginning of the year, the IT stocks had dominated the ranking lists. By mid-2000 however these stocks were under heavy fire and the more traditional types of companies started looking good again. Despite actually making profits.

The portfolio built up during this time was very low on IT stocks but otherwise quite balanced. Discretionary, staples, energy, industrials, financials and materials were all represented. This is also the reason for the outperformance that we showed late this year.

The markets started dropping fast in late 2000, but the decline was primarily lead by the tech stocks. Since we had near zero exposure to this theme already, we didn't experience the loss that the index felt. We didn't really gain much either though.

On each rebalance, some stocks went out of the portfolio. Since the index is now below water, no new purchases could be made and our cash holding kept increasing. By the end of the year, we were almost entirely in cash.

After a very tough year, we ended up with a positive performance of almost 10%, while the index lost about the same amount. It may seem as a defeat to end up with a measly 10%, but that's really quite a respectable return and in particular in a year as tough as this. Remember that we're using the broad S&P 500 index as our benchmark here. Most people at the time still held onto their IT stocks and those took significantly worse losses than 10%.

The Motorola trade in Figure 13-6 shows how we entered this stock after the strong move up during late 1999. We bought the stock in December 1999 and it all looked well for a few months. As the stock started falling in March, we followed it down until it dipped below its 100 day moving average. That was the exit signal in this case and that's when we got out. As it turns out, we were lucky this time since it made a large gap down just a few days after.

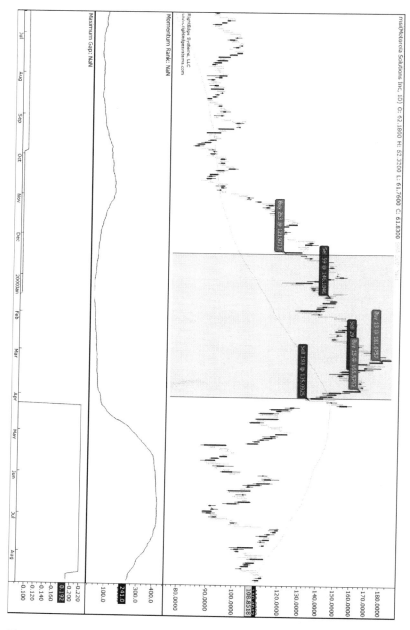

Figure 13-6 Motorola

If you look closely at the momentum rank in the middle pane, you'll also see that it came up to the critical level at the same time as the stock dropped below the moving average. So in this particular case, we would have exited either way with either the moving average rule or the rank rule. Note how we closed out on a dip. A few days after that exit, it probably felt like a very bad idea. The price jumped right up and even popped up above the moving average. And then, just when you would have beaten your head in the keyboard for selling too early, the stock made a surprise 22% gap down.

You'll never enter at the best place and you'll never exit at the best place. But the good news is that you really don't have to. A momentum strategy like this works just fine without trying to time the exact peaks and bottoms.

We're now mostly in cash but we've got a safe head start on the index from the start of 1999. Figure 13-7 shows the development of our momentum strategy compared to the S&P 500 total return index from the start. We had a slow year, but so far so good.

Table 13-4 Results 2000

	Momentum Strategy	S&P 500 Total Return Index
Return 2000	9.6%	-8.1%
Max Drawdown 2000	-15.4%	-16.6%
Annualized Return Since 1999	24.3%	5.4%
Max Drawdown since 1999	-15.4%	-16.6%

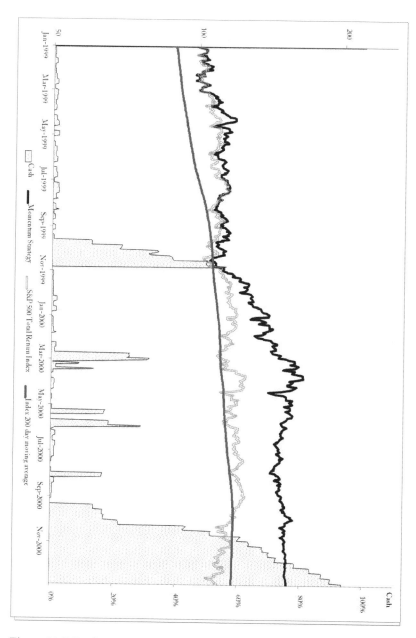

Figure 13-7 Performance 1999 to 2000

2001

Moving into 2001, we had a surprisingly well behaved scale-out of the markets behind us. When we start this year, we only hold two stocks. Two brave soldiers survived the onslaught last year. This means that we start the year holding a portfolio almost entirely in cash. United Health Group and Entergy Corp made it past the New Year's celebrations, but two weeks into January they were both sold as well. After that, no trading was done the entire year.

Table 13-5 Initial Portfolio, 2001

Name	Weight	Sector
UnitedHealth Group Inc	3.1%	Health Care
Entergy Corp	3.3%	Utilities

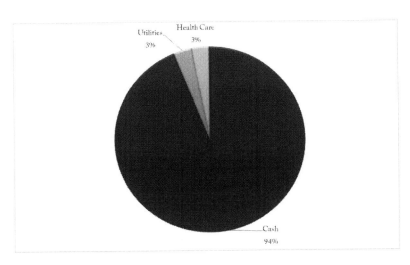

Figure 13-8 Initial Sector Allocation, 2001

While this year was very dramatic for most people, as far as our strategy is concerned it was a very boring year. We took a loss of less than a percent in January before our only two stocks were closed. After that, we're flat lined. This is again something which is very easy in theory but more difficult in reality. Looking back at a long track record, it makes perfect sense to stay away this year. In reality, most people would be very tempted to trade.

Someone might wonder why we don't go short in such a year. Why not find the stocks that fall the most, and short them? A reversed momentum approach. The answer is simple. Such a strategy has very low chance of success. Shorting is much more difficult, and dangerous, than it may seem. Very few people make money shorting stocks.

Those stocks that kept falling for the past month may suddenly make an enormous jump up. The propensity for volatility expansion is dramatically higher in a bear market. Don't be tempted to trade such a market. Don't buy stocks and don't short them. There's a slaughter going on out there and your job is to survive it. There will be opportunities to make profits, but now is not the time.

If you're looking for action, you're likely to get it. Those looking for action are unlikely to find profits though. Learning when to sit tight and keep risks to a minimum is a key part is becoming an investment professional.

Figure 13-10 shows how one of our surviving stocks in early 2011 faired. United Health Group had been performing admirably in the face of a falling market. Below the price pane, you can see the index itself and how it kept falling. Very few stocks can keep moving up while the market is declining like that.

Even this amazingly strong stock started declining in December 2000 and by the rebalance time early in 2001, it was trading below its 100 day moving average. That's our exit cue and time to sell it. Since the index itself is clearly in bear mode, we're not replacing it and before the end of January we're holding nothing but greenbacks.

Table 13-6 Results 2001

	Momentum Strategy	S&P 500 Total Return Index
Return 2001	-0.7%	-10.9%
Max Drawdown 2001	-0.8%	-29.1%
Annualized Return Since 1999	15.3%	-0.7%
Max Drawdown since 1999	-15.4%	-35.7%

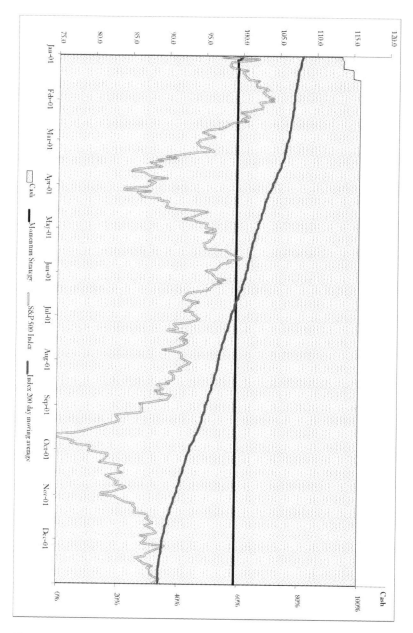

Figure 13-9 Performance, 2001

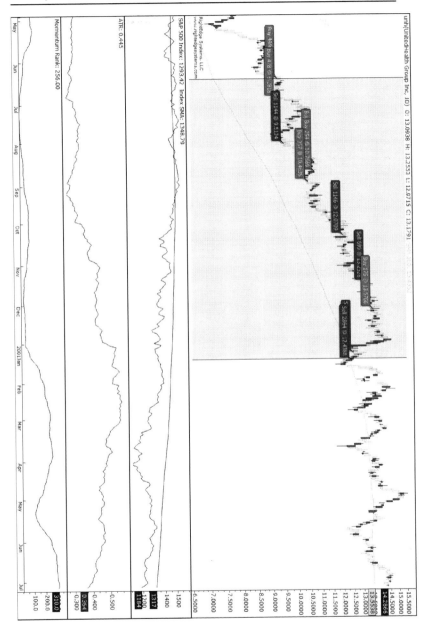

Figure 13-10 United Health Group

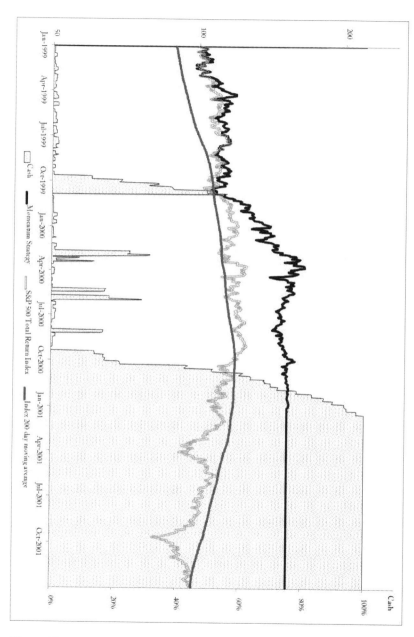

Figure 13-11 Performance 1999-2001

2002

Going into 2002, we hold exactly zero stocks. The entire portfolio is in good old cash. In this context, it's important to understand that cash in these situations should never actually be held in real cash. It's just an expression. I'm not just referring to the obvious fact that you don't keep your portfolio in physical dollar bills, stored in silver attaché case chained to your wrist. You shouldn't keep this cash in a bank account either.

The problem with cash, even in a bank account, is that it's unsecure. If your bank or broker suddenly blows up, the cash is the problem. At least if your cash holdings are larger than your government's depositor guarantees. Back in 2002 many people may still may have held the view that banks don't blow up, but more recent years have taught us otherwise. If your bank or broker goes the way of the dodo, you'll most likely get all your securities back. At least after some delays and possibly some legal fights, but you're still likely to get that back. Securities are registered in your name and are separated from any potential bankruptcy claims. The cash on the other hand goes poof the instant your bank or broker fails.

What you do in reality is to place excess cash in money market instruments or even treasuries, depending on how long time you expect to be keeping it in 'cash'. This is just common sense.

While there was not very much trading activity in 2002, we had one interesting phase. It's not like we stayed liquid the whole year. In March the index raised a periscope above the water line and as it moved higher than the 200 day moving average, we of course have to start buying.

The portfolio table here is not from the beginning of 2002. That would have been an empty table and looked quite silly, wouldn't it? No, Table 13-7 shows the list of stocks that we bought in March 2002, when the index was starting to really improve.

Table 13-7 March 2002 Portfolio

Name	Weight	Sector
American Airlines Group Inc	2.5%	Industrials
Boeing Co	3.4%	Industrials
Brunswick Corp	4.6%	Consumer Discretionary

Black & Decker Corp	4.2%	Consumer Discretionary
Big Lots Inc	3.2%	Consumer Discretionary
Ball Corp	5.2%	Materials
Cooper Tire & Rubber Co	3.3%	Consumer Discretionary
Deluxe Corp	5.6%	Industrials
Darden Restaurants Inc	2.9%	Consumer Discretionary
Ecolab Inc	5.4%	Materials
Golden West Financial Corp	5.0%	Financials
Goodrich Corp	4.3%	Industrials
W W Grainger Inc	4.3%	Industrials
Nordstrom Inc	3.2%	Consumer Discretionary
KB Home	2.3%	Consumer Discretionary
L Brands Inc	3.1%	Consumer Discretionary
Masco Corp	3.4%	Industrials
Mcdermott International Inc	2.4%	Energy
Parker Hannifin Corp	4.1%	Industrials
PulteGroup Inc	3.0%	Consumer Discretionary
Ryder System Inc	4.5%	Industrials
Rockwell Automation Inc	3.4%	Industrials
Siebel Systems Inc	1.7%	Information Technology
Tiffany & Co	3.0%	Consumer Discretionary
T. Rowe Price Group Inc	3.9%	Financials
Sabre Holdings Corp	3.3%	Information Technology
Xerox Corp	2.5%	Information Technology

This portfolio has heavy weights of industrials and consumer discretionary stocks. The tech stocks are still not forgiven by the markets and we only held 8% of those. This seems like a reasonable portfolio, given the market conditions. It's not a very aggressive stance but it's not like it's full of defensive utilities and staples either.

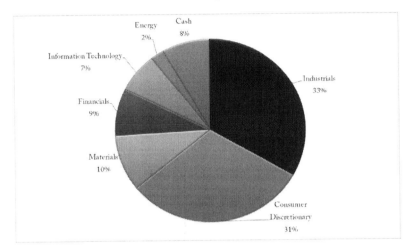

Figure 13-12 March 2002 Sector Allocation

It was a nice attempt, but unfortunately it failed. The index didn't stay long above the moving average. After only a few weeks, the index said bye bye to the average and the two barely saw each other for the remainder of the year.

As a result, our portfolio got slowly reduced through the rebalancing process. The heaviest index casualties were taken by the tech sector and our stocks didn't actually do that poorly. The long time it took to scale out is a testament to how well they held up under the heavy market pressure. We kept slowly selling stocks as they went below their moving average, made too large gaps or failed to meet the other criteria. It took all the way to July before we were back to an all cash portfolio once again.

The performance on the year was quite boring, despite buying a fully loaded portfolio in the middle of a bear market. All in all, we ended up losing about 3%, while the index lost a whopping 22%.

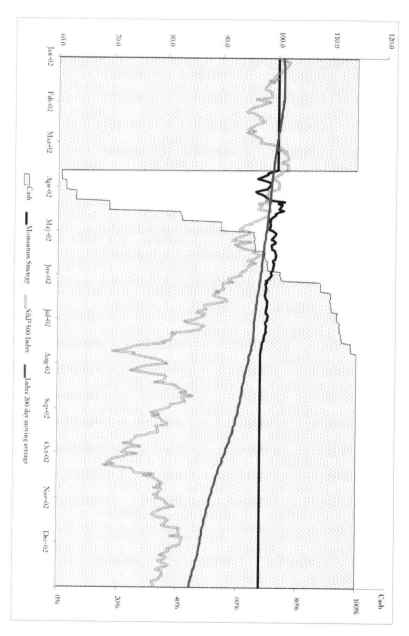

Figure 13-13 Performance, 2002

Another year of mostly sitting on our hands, but remember that relative to most people, the performance was very good. Losing a few percent while the markets are in disarray is nothing to be ashamed of.

What happened in Figure 13-14 is more or less what happened to all the stocks bought in 2002. The bear market was beginning to slow down and the index had been moving sideways long enough for it to briefly move up over the long term moving average. That gave us a green light to buy new stocks, and buy we did.

The stocks, in this case Boeing, also had a nice recovery and was starting to look quite constructive again. We entered the stock in March and by mid-April we were already out of it. The next round of selloffs in the index didn't take long to start and the entry was, in retrospect, very poorly timed. Well, you can't win them all.

After four years we have a rather odd performance curve, as you'll see in Figure 13-15. At first all seemed just fine. We made strong returns early on and showed a sizable outperformance against the index. But once the bear market started, we went into cash and stayed in cash almost the whole time.

Table 13-8 Results 2002

	Momentum Strategy	S&P 500 Total Return Index
Return 2002	-3.0%	-22.1%
Max Drawdown 2002	-4.2%	-33.0%
Annualized Return Since 1999	10.4%	-6.8%
Max Drawdown since 1999	-15.4%	-47.4%

Now we had two years of doing practically nothing and just holding cash. What kind of strategy is that?

I know it's tough to do. Most traders are looking for action and have very itchy fingers. You're watching the market decline and you want to jump in, either to sell short or to buy cheap. Trust me, in these market conditions, it's a very bad idea. Very few people make money from the stock markets in such conditions. Oh, in retrospect everyone knows what should have been done. But in reality, these are very dangerous times and if you're able to simply preserve your capital while everyone else is losing, you'll end up far ahead.

This is not the time to take on risk. Sit tight and hold on.

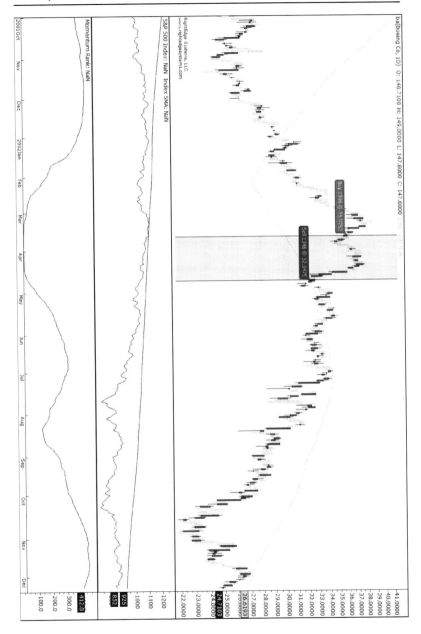

Figure 13-14 Boeing

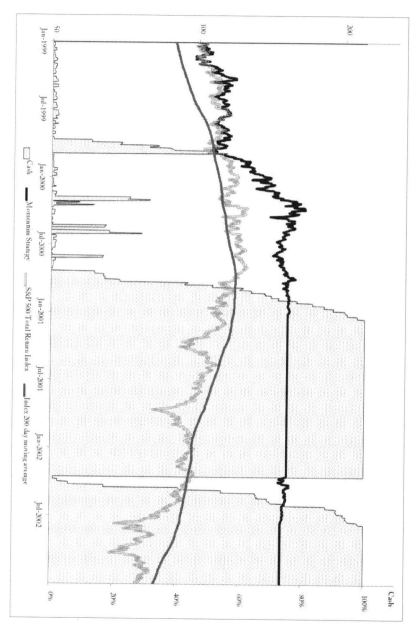

Figure 13-15 Performance 1999-2002

2003

After the two difficult years we had behind us, most equity momentum traders have already quit the game. The best we can say about the past two years is that we didn't lose much money, while most others did. There's another strategy that could have performed that just as well, and it's called "Just Stay Away". For our momentum strategy to make any sense, we need to see some returns soon. Beating the index in a bear market is simple. We need to see how it performs when things improve.

At the start of 2003, our portfolio is identical to the one we had going into the previous year. That is, we don't hold a single stock. In the first couple of months, that felt like a very good idea. The market dropped 10% by early March and we're still flat lined. But then the market starts turning up, making rapid gains without us. No need to worry though, that moving average is closing in fast. Finally in April, the index gives the green light to start building up a new portfolio.

The portfolio in Table 13-9 shows which stocks we bought at this time. It's all in all quite a balanced portfolio, but with a clear overweight in health care. While this portfolio changed a bit over the course of the year, it showed a very interesting performance.

Table 13-9 April 2003 Portfolio

Name	Weight	Sector
Adobe Systems Inc	2.6%	Information Technology
Aetna Inc	3.8%	Health Care
Allergan Inc	4.6%	Health Care
Amgen Inc	4.6%	Health Care
Apollo Education Group Inc	3.8%	Consumer Discretionary
Best Buy Co Inc	2.4%	Consumer Discretionary
Becton Dickinson and Co	4.0%	Health Care
Brown-Forman Corp	6.4%	Consumer Staples
Avis Budget Group Inc	3.0%	Industrials
eBay Inc	4.6%	Information Technology

Fluor Corp	3.2% Industrials
Guidant LLC	3.2% Health Care
Hasbro Inc	4.2% Consumer Discretionary
Mattel Inc	4.0% Consumer Discretionary
Medimmune LLC	2.9% Health Care
Marathon Oil Corp	5.0% Energy
Nike Inc	3.9% Consumer Discretionary
Public Service Enterprise Group Inc	5.3% Utilities
Progressive Corp	4.7% Financials
Pall Corp	3.8% Industrials
Reebok International Ltd	4.5% Consumer Discretionary
Starbucks Corp	3.4% Consumer Discretionary
St. Jude Medical Inc	4.6% Health Care
Yahoo! Inc	2.6% Information Technology
Zimmer Holdings Inc	3.7% Health Care

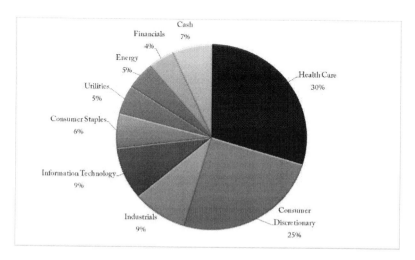

Figure 13-16 Sector Allocation, April 2003

As opposed to last year, this time when the index breached the moving average it just kept powering on. The cross was made by mid-April and after that the index just kept increasing the distance to the average. Our momentum strategy did quite well too. At first it merely copied the index, keeping an equal footing for a few months. The index was gaining nicely, so copying the index performance in such a phase is quite alright.

Then in the late summer, our stocks started accelerating. At that time, we already had a 20% profit on the year, but that wasn't enough. For the first time in years, there's optimism back in the markets. People are buying stocks as if they're about to go out of print. This is exactly the kind of environment where momentum investing shines.

The index was left behind in the dust and while it ended at a very respectable +28% on the year, we cashed in on a whopping +42%. Not bad at all. Except of course if you called it quits after those past couple of mediocre years and stopped trading.

This year we knocked a few balls out of the park. In Figure 13-18 you see what happened after we bought Sanmina in June of 2003. Before it was sold early 2004, it more than doubled for us. Also note all those trades along the way, shown in that figure. You should have gotten used to seeing this by now. All these trades are the small rebalances done to compensate for changing volatility. These trades are all done to try to keep risks constant, as the position risk always keeps changing.

This is exactly the kind of trade we want to see with a momentum strategy. In a good year, we get several of these top performing stocks.

At the end of 2002 it looked like our whole strategy was to just hold cash. We had two years of almost flat performance at that time. After this year, it should be clear how the long term strategy works. Without clear rules for when to enter and exit the market, you'll risk both losing too much in bear markets and missing the inevitable recovery rally.

Table 13-10 Results 2003

	Momentum Strategy	S&P 500 Total Return Index
Return 2003	41.8%	28.7%
Max Drawdown 2003	-7.2%	-13.8%
Annualized Return Since 1999	16.1%	-0.6%
Max Drawdown since 1999	-15.4%	-47.4%

We entered at very good timing here and as the market recovered, we were in the right sectors and the right stocks. Now after five years, we can show a very substantial outperformance against the market and very strong absolute returns.

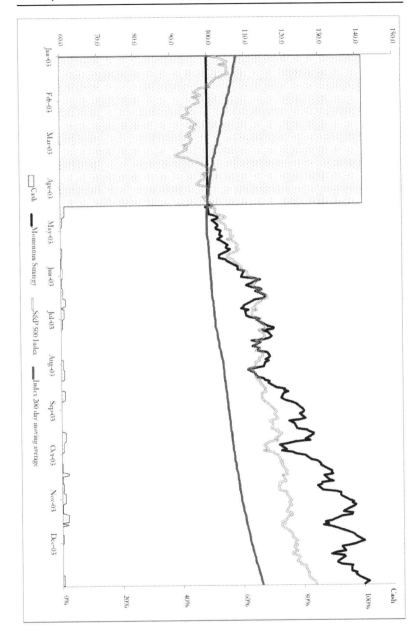

Figure 13-17 Performance, 2003

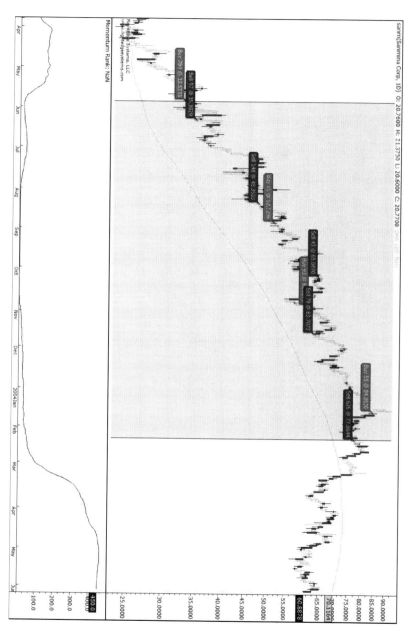

Figure 13-18 Sanmina Corp

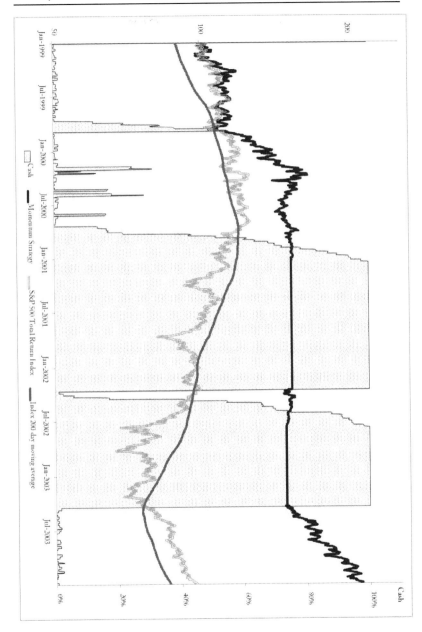

Figure 13-19 Performance 1999-2003

2004

Finally we have a bit more of a normal start of a year. In January of 2004 the Dot Com Crash is long gone from memory and the rally is on. We just had over half a year of stellar performance and the markets don't seem to want to stop rising. As the year starts, we have a very broad portfolio of 27 stocks, covering all sectors except financials. Now we're even back in the tech stocks with an allocation of 28%. Last year we made outsized gains, so the spirits are high and we're fully loaded.

Table 13-11 Initial Portfolio, 2004

Name	Weight	Sector
Sanmina Corp	2.2%	Information Technology
Humana Inc	4.0%	Health Care
Freeport-McMoRan Inc	2.7%	Materials
Louisiana-Pacific Corp	3.6%	Materials
Georgia-Pacific LLC	4.7%	Materials
Advanced Micro Devices Inc	2.3%	Information Technology
Nordstrom Inc	4.3%	Consumer Discretionary
Motorola Solutions Inc	3.2%	Information Technology
Freeport-Mcmoran Corp	4.2%	Materials
Texas Instruments Inc	3.1%	Information Technology
Alcatel-Lucent USA Inc	2.3%	Telecommunication Services
Yahoo! Inc	3.1%	Information Technology
PMC-Sierra Inc	2.1%	Information Technology
United States Steel Corp	4.3%	Materials
PulteGroup Inc	4.0%	Consumer Discretionary
Broadcom Corp	2.3%	Information Technology
Reynolds American Inc	4.7%	Consumer Staples
Siebel Systems Inc	3.0%	Information Technology
AES Corp	3.0%	Utilities
Teradyne Inc	2.6%	Information Technology
International Game Technology	4.6%	Consumer Discretionary
Nextel Communications Inc	3.7%	Telecommunication

	Services
Autodesk Inc	3.7% Information Technology
Altria Group Inc	7.3% Consumer Staples
Zimmer Holdings Inc	5.6% Health Care
Schneider Electric IT Corp	3.3% Energy
Rockwell Automation Inc	5.3% Industrials

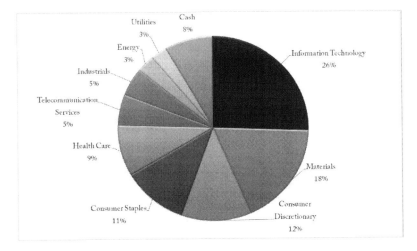

Figure 13-20 Initial Sector Allocation, 2004

Most of 2004 was nowhere near as fun as we had the previous year. What we got here was quite high portfolio volatility, with the bottom line moving swiftly up to +7%, only to lose it all. For several months this choppy behavior keeps going, swinging up and down. Then in August, the market starts dropping again and we're already behind the index.

The market dropped below the moving average in late summer, signaling a halt to new purchases. Our portfolio dropped in value further and started scaling down exposure as stocks were sold in the rebalancing. At the worst, we had a 9% loss in August while the market only saw a maximum loss of 9%. That's not a fun situation to be in. Having just regained confidence in this strategy last year, this is another time when it's understandable to doubt the whole thing. We kept trading all year, doing all this work, and now in August all we have to show for it is a volatile, underperforming portfolio with a near double digit loss.

What you have to remember is that momentum investing is a long term approach. It's a way of beating the markets in the long run. Some years it works, some years it doesn't. Over time, it's always done much better than the equity markets and it has always produced a handsome return. Let's stick with our strategy a little longer and see what happens.

That reading in August turned out to be the worst we saw that year. In fact, after that, we saw an incredible rally. Starting at -9% in early August, we took off like a rocket ship. The index came up again over the moving average, allowing us to rebuy a fully loaded portfolio and it turned out to be the right stocks.

From here, we quickly advanced in a rally that lasted for the rest of the year. Come December, we had a gain of 14%, both beating the index and providing a strong absolute return. Some may think that 14% is a horribly poor return. This is usually an attitude that's popular on anonymous trading forums, where everyone claims to make hundreds or even thousands of percent per year. Those figures are all fine for trash talking on anonymous online forums, but in the real world very few people can compound at 14% over longer periods of time.

The Autodesk position in Figure 13-22 shows a great long term position. In case you're wondering why there are no rebalancing trades shown, it's simply that I removed the labels to make it easier to see the chart. Over such a long period, you'd get so many trade labels that you could barely see the price anymore.

This position was opened in December of 2003, held the entire 2004 and sold by the end of January 2005. In this period, the price tripled, greatly contributing to our portfolio performance during this time.

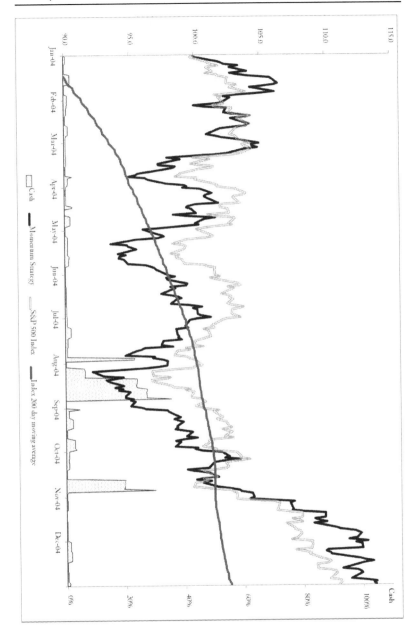

Figure 13-21 Performance, 2004

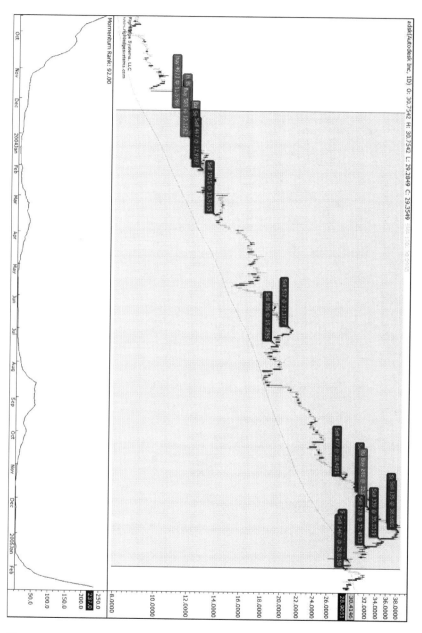

Figure 13-22 Autodesk

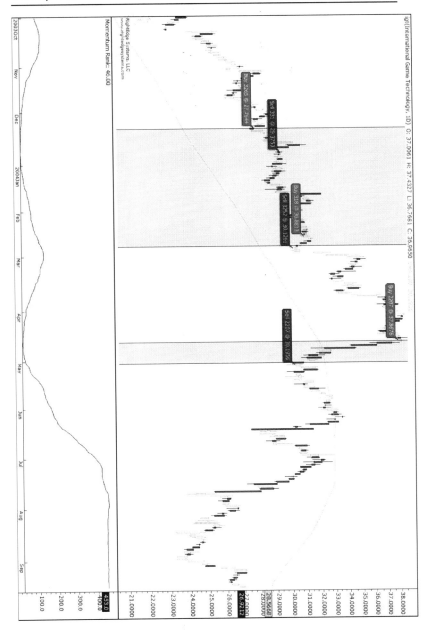

Figure 13-23 International Game Technology

Not all trades are as fun as Autodesk of course. Even in good years, there are plenty of bad trades. The IGT trade shown in Figure 13-23 is a good example. We had previously traded this stock in late 2003 with ok results. Not great, but we exited with a small profit. By April of 2004, IGT were one of the highest ranked momentum stocks and we bought it again. This time, it simply tanked the day after we bought it. The share price fell right back down, right through the moving average and at the next rebalance we exited with a loss.

This happens all the time but it's nothing to worry about. That's the cost of doing business. It was a valid trade, but it just didn't work out. We still did well on the year.

By this time we're very far ahead of the index and our momentum strategy has proven its worth. You should start to see the long term pattern by now; outperform in bull markets, defend in bear markets.

If you had invested $100 in an index tracker at the start of 1999, you would now have about $106 dollars. If on the other hand you would have invested that in this momentum approach, you would now have more than doubled your money already.

Table 13-12 Results 2004

	Momentum Strategy	S&P 500 Total Return Index
Return 2004	13.7%	10.9%
Max Drawdown 2004	-13.5%	-7.4%
Annualized Return Since 1999	15.7%	1.3%
Max Drawdown since 1999	-15.4%	-47.4%

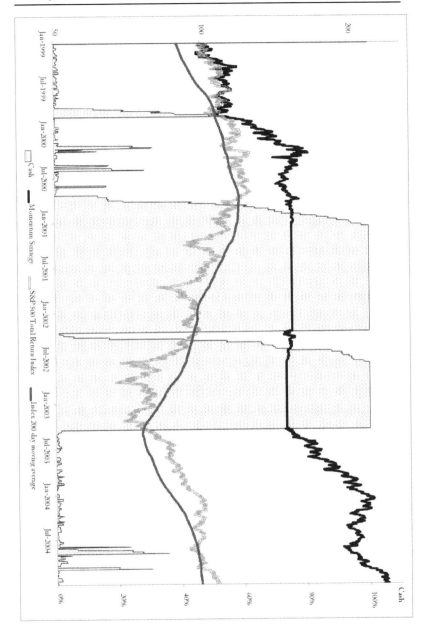

Figure 13-24 Performance 1999-2004

2005

In 2005, the tech stocks are back in vogue again and in a big way. In fact, half of our initial portfolio this year time is in the IT sector. That heavy allocation to a single sector makes a very clear statement. This means that there's a major trend going on in that particular space, and we're in on it. The tech stocks have gone from being the pariah of the stock markets to the main driver again. Apart from the tech stocks, we've got significant exposure to industrials, discretionary and energy sectors.

Table 13-13 Initial Portfolio, 2005

Name	Weight	Sector
Autodesk Inc	3.9%	Information Technology
Apple Inc	3.1%	Information Technology
Energy Future Holdings Corp	5.2%	Energy
Norfolk Southern Corp	5.5%	Industrials
Black & Decker Corp	6.5%	Consumer Discretionary
PACCAR Inc	4.6%	Industrials
Transocean Ltd	3.8%	Energy
KB Home	3.5%	Consumer Discretionary
Brunswick Corp	4.8%	Consumer Discretionary
Adobe Systems Inc	4.2%	Information Technology
Franklin Resources Inc	6.6%	Financials
Gateway Inc	2.3%	Information Technology
Citrix Systems Inc	3.4%	Information Technology
Advanced Micro Devices Inc	2.7%	Information Technology
eBay Inc	4.6%	Information Technology
Comverse Technology Inc	2.8%	Information Technology
Monster Worldwide Inc	4.1%	Information

		Technology
QLogic Corp	3.2%	Information Technology
Andrew LLC	3.1%	Information Technology
Oracle America Inc	2.8%	Information Technology
Parker Hannifin Corp	5.7%	Industrials
NVIDIA Corp	2.8%	Information Technology
Compuware Corp	2.4%	Information Technology
NCR Corp	4.8%	Information Technology
Williams Companies Inc	3.6%	Energy

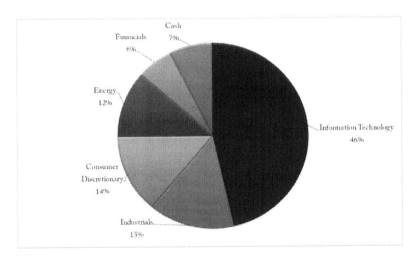

Figure 13-25 Initial Allocation, 2005

Last year saw a multi-month rally by the end, with our portfolio showing significant gains from August to December. Having had such an incredible few months behind us, everyone's got high expectations going into 2005. This year however, we get a tough start. Already in the first couple of days we drop a few percent. Not too worrying, but it's never fun to be down four percent in the first week of the year. Well, we've seen volatility before so perhaps this doesn't worry us too much at the time.

But two weeks later, when January is almost over and we find ourselves in a six percent hole it's not so fun anymore. These situations may look trivial when you've got a long term performance chart in front of you and look back at what appears to be minor blips. They're a whole different thing when they actually happen with real money, when you have no idea how the future will play out. It's only natural that you stop and think about what will happen if you keep going at the same rate. If every month this year would end up losing six percent, you would lose 50% in a year. It's not healthy to make such calculations, but we all do it.

What happened here was that the market recovered and the stocks that we held recovered the fastest. As the market normalized and moved up for the next couple of months, we saw a strong performance boost in our portfolio. From the bottom at -6%, we rallied all the way up to +7% in March. Rides like this can be tough from a psychological point of view. If you had $100,000 of your hard earned cash in this portfolio at the start of the year, you would first have lost $6,000 in the first couple of weeks and then gained $11,000 in the next couple of months. Now you're on top of the world and back to doing compound return math. You just made 11% in two months, and if you continue like that you would make 87% in a year. That's $87,000 if you had $100,000 to start with.

It's tempting to think like that, but try not to. It will never play out like that. Not anywhere near it. Not the -40% that you feared in January and not the +87% that you dreamed of in March.

This year continued to be a roller coaster. As the markets pulled back a little bit in the second quarter, our stocks continued to demonstrate their high beta. From the peak reading of +7%, we fell all the way back down to -6% by mid-year. These situations are extremely frustrating. You've seen decent profits on the year, and given it all up. You've worked all year with your momentum models, calculations, rebalancing, and you've got only losses to show for it.

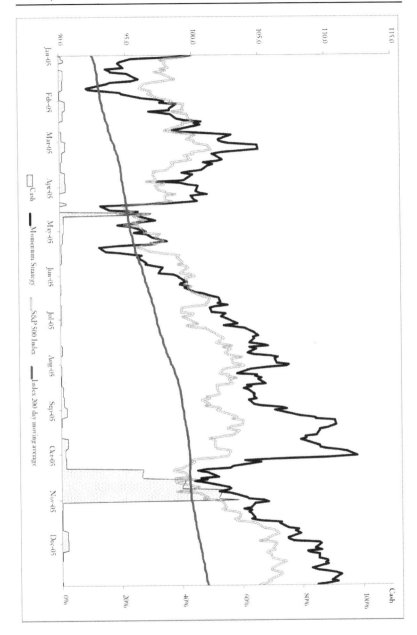

Figure 13-26 Performance, 2005

The roller coaster ride of 2005 is far from over though. This year was a nail biter, with a strong second rally from May to September that saw a move in our portfolio from -6% to +13%. That's over 20% in a few months. Not bad at all. The only problem is, after that, there was a big loss in short period of time. Our returns plummeted down from +13% to zero in a matter of weeks. The move was not that dramatic in the index itself but our portfolio consisted of high beta stocks and took a severe short term beating.

The index once again saw the underbelly of the 200 day moving average and we're no longer allowed to replace outgoing stocks. The cash starts building up and come November we're down to less than half speed. Over half of our portfolio is held in plain old cash.

This, as it turns out, is exactly the wrong time to reduce stocks. That's very easy to say after the fact. The index dipped below the average, only to emerge soon after and rally on. We're left in the dust, since we're only in the market with one foot. Amazingly, we're able to keep up with the index as it rallies, even though we're on such low exposure level. The stocks that were left in the portfolio did significantly better than the index and held an equal footing with the market.

Looking at the poor timing of the October scale-out in Figure 13-26 it would be fair to wonder if we shouldn't change the parameters. After all, if we had used a 220 day moving average this horrible timing would have been averted. It's an easy trap to fall into. To change the parameters based on hindsight knowledge.

My intention with this book is to present realism. I want to show how things work in reality and I refuse to show an optimized historic back test with incredible results just to sell some more books. The realistic situation is that these things happen, and much worse things still. Making the strategy appear much more profitable and giving it magical timing abilities would be easy in hindsight, but that wouldn't help anyone reading this book.

At least this year ended fairly well, after many swings in performance and a scale-down at the worst time. The index itself ended the year at about +5%, while we finished at +9%. Still not a bad return. Over time, the outperformance against the index adds up. Consistency is what we're aiming for.

Table 13-14 Results 2005

	Momentum Strategy	S&P 500 Total Return Index
Return 2005	9.3%	4.9%
Max Drawdown 2005	-11.4%	-7.0%
Annualized Return Since 1999	14.8%	1.8%
Max Drawdown since 1999	-15.4%	-47.4%

The Anthem trade in Figure 13-27 demonstrates a frustrating situation that will occur quite often with this strategy. We bought into this stock after a strong run up, as usual. Note in the lower pane how the stock keeps climbing the ranking list. When we bought the stock, it was ranked number 12 among all the 500 stocks in the index. Right after we bought it however, the momentum was all but gone. It didn't fall down. It's just that it stopped moving. Several months later, we finally exit with absolutely nothing to show for a near four month position. To make matters worse, right after we sell it, the stock decides it's time to start moving up again. Of course, by then the rank of this stock has worsen enough to push it off the top list and now we're replacing it with something completely unrelated.

Well, again this is the cost of doing business. You're not going to have all winners. Always keep in mind that any individual position is absolutely irrelevant. We're in this for the portfolio, not for the position. This strategy, as with most professional trading strategies, is not designed to win on every trade. It's designed to win in the long run, on a portfolio basis.

Aetna on the other hand, in Figure 13-28 was a more encouraging trade. Here we bought with very good timing, albeit by luck, just before the stock started a new leg up.

So far so good. We're seven years in and we've got a huge lead on the index. This particular year we showed more or less market performance, but given our existing head start that's not all that bad.

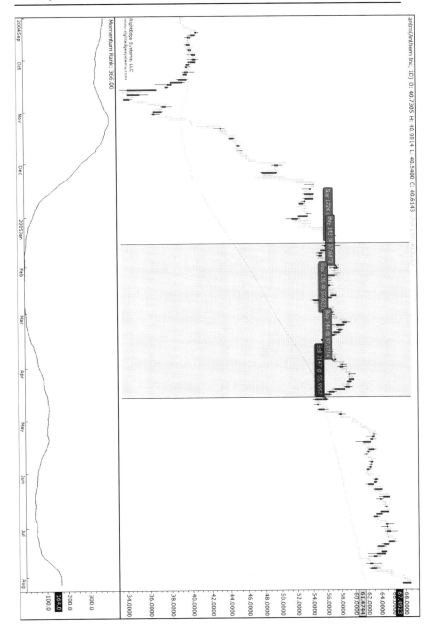

Figure 13-27 Anthem

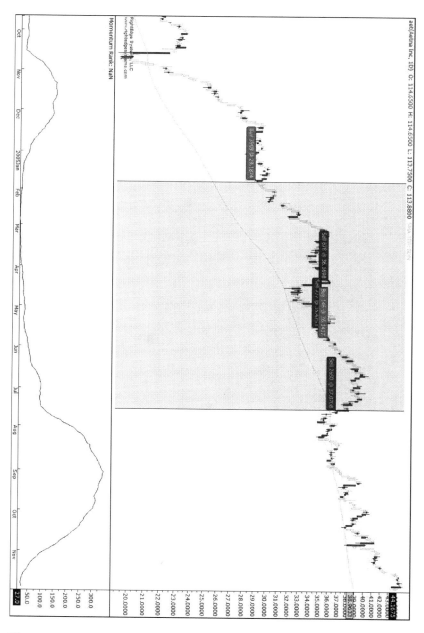

Figure 13-28 Aetna

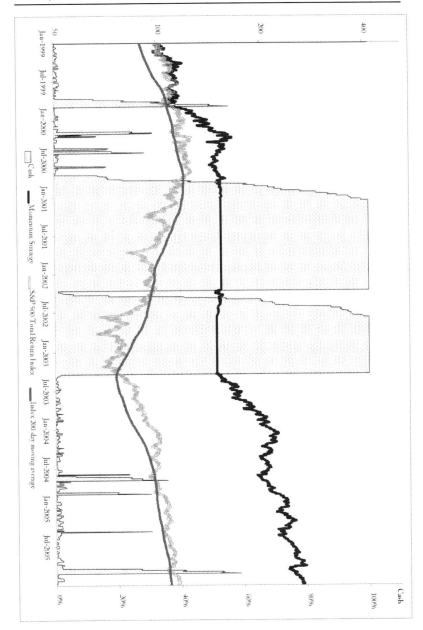

Figure 13-29 Performance 1999-2005

2006

We just left a tough but profitable year behind us. It was a nail biter, but at least we ended in double digits. As this year starts out, we're still a bit heavy in tech, but still reasonably diversified. We've got large allocations to financials, industrials, health care and discretionary. Note the lack of utilities and telecom. These two sectors are rarely given much attention in momentum investing, as they haven't demonstrated any real ability to produce momentum stocks. The staples sector is also missing from the starting lineup but that sector can from time to time show great performers.

Table 13-15 Initial Portfolio, 2006

Name	Weight	Sector
Express Scripts Holding Co	3.6%	Health Care
E*TRADE Financial Corp	3.3%	Financials
Advanced Micro Devices Inc	3.2%	Information Technology
Robert Half	4.6%	Industrials
BJ Services Company LLC	3.3%	Energy
Medimmune LLC	3.1%	Health Care
Norfolk Southern Corp	5.2%	Industrials
Aon PLC	5.1%	Financials
Applied Biosystems Inc	4.9%	Health Care
Freeport-McMoRan Inc	3.8%	Materials
Apple Inc	3.9%	Information Technology
Novell Inc	3.2%	Information Technology
Freeport-Mcmoran Corp	3.2%	Materials
Burlington Northern Santa Fe	5.7%	Industrials
JDS Uniphase Corp	1.7%	Information Technology
NVIDIA Corp	2.8%	Information Technology
Progressive Corp	5.0%	Financials
Citrix Systems Inc	4.6%	Information Technology

Ciena Corp	2.0% Information Technology
Adobe Systems Inc	3.1% Information Technology
Gilead Sciences Inc	3.0% Health Care
Janus Capital Group Inc	4.0% Financials
NetApp Inc	3.3% Information Technology
Starbucks Corp	4.2% Consumer Discretionary
Circuit City Stores Inc	3.8% Consumer Discretionary
Monster Worldwide Inc	3.9% Information Technology

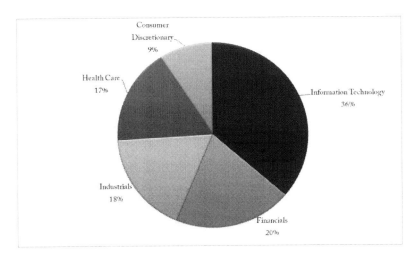

Figure 13-30 Initial Sector Allocation, 2006

This year started really well. It was an amazing run from the start of the year, all the way up to early May. At that point, we already had a profit of 19%. Things looked good. It often does before the trouble starts. This turned out to be a very disappointing year for momentum investing. The sectors that had been the top performers for over a year now suddenly plunged down. We took losses all around and the portfolio value quickly declined.

To make matters worse, we had terrible luck with timing the exposure scaling during the summer. The index dropped below the moving average in June and we quickly reduced exposure. Multiple stocks were sold on each rebalance, and in early July we held 60% cash. Just then, a bear market rally comes along and pushes us back into the market. The index poked its head over the waterline, trigger buys across the board. No sooner had we finished buying stocks than the market again started falling. Now with high exposure we took a swift loss before scaling down again as the index drops below the average for the second time. And of course, just as we're down to only half exposure again, the market recovers and starts a rebound. It's hard not to take it personally.

This time, the momentum approach really struggled. We spent the second part of the year underperforming the market, slowly creeping up but not anywhere near as much as the market. So what happened here? How come the momentum approach suddenly stopped working?

The initial decline is clear. The momentum sectors took a hit, and our beta heavy strategy took a bigger hit. That's to be expected from time to time. It's more concerning that we failed to show any real performance in the second part of the year. Well, this is just the way things turn out at times. In this particular period in time, the momentum approach didn't work very well. We bought several stocks that had had a good run for a while, but after we bought them they didn't perform as well anymore. Most of them were sold with small profits or small losses, and replaced with other stocks that didn't make any real waves either.

Don't expect any strategy to work well all of the time.

The Office Depot trade in Figure 13-32 demonstrates what happened to many positions around mid-year and why the portfolio performance fell back so hard. In this case, the position which was opened in March did quite well for a couple of months before it started falling back down. As practically all other stocks fell too, the ranking of this stock remained high relative to the rest. That's why it took so long before it was sold.

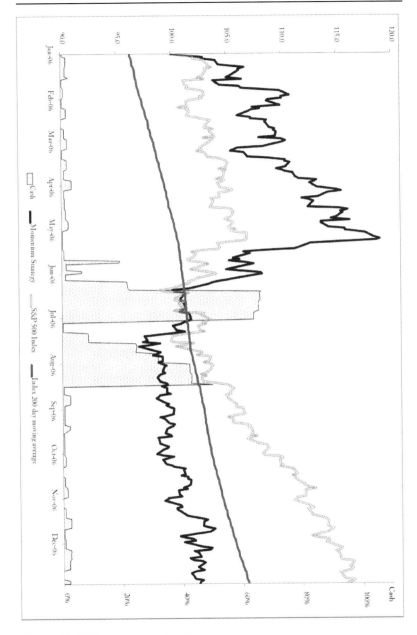

Figure 13-31 Performance, 2006

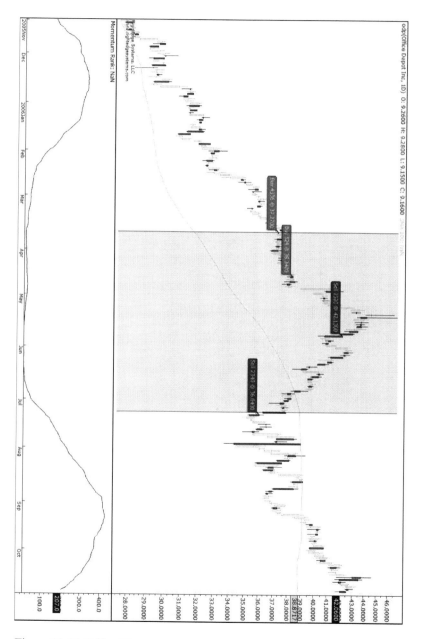

Figure 13-32 Office Depot

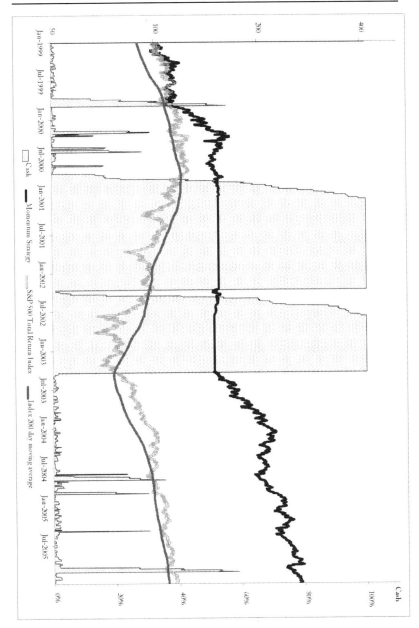

Figure 13-33 Performance 1999-2006

Table 13-16 Results 2006

	Momentum Strategy	S&P 500 Total Return Index
Return 2006	2.4%	15.8%
Max Drawdown 2006	-18.5%	-7.5%
Annualized Return Since 1999	13.1%	3.4%
Max Drawdown since 1999	-18.5%	-47.4%

It wasn't a very fun year and even though we ended a little better than even, we gave up a nice early year performance and we lost big relatively to the index. Keep that long term chart in Figure 13-33 in mind. This strategy is for the long haul. Any given year, anything can happen. In the long run, we win.

2007

After having had a shaky 2006, we really need to see some performance soon to regain confidence in the strategy. The end of last year was embarrassing. This is again a year where the tech stocks have done quite well lately, and therefore we're heavily allocated to that sector. In fact, the initial portfolio this year is completely dominated by two sectors. The tech sector together with the discretionary sector covers almost 85% of our portfolio. Now that's quite an aggressive posture.

Table 13-17 Initial Portfolio, 2007

Name	Weight	Sector
Apple Inc	3.6%	Information Technology
Adobe Systems Inc	3.7%	Information Technology
Amazon.com Inc	3.7%	Consumer Discretionary
Allegheny Technologies Inc	2.9%	Materials
Autozone Inc	6.9%	Consumer Discretionary
Big Lots Inc	2.8%	Consumer Discretionary
BMC Software Inc	5.0%	Information Technology
CBRE Group Inc	3.0%	Financials
Celgene Corp	3.2%	Health Care
Coach Inc	4.1%	Consumer Discretionary
Cisco Systems Inc	4.4%	Information Technology
Eastman Kodak Co	4.1%	Information Technology
Goldman Sachs Group Inc	5.0%	Financials
Goodyear Tire & Rubber Co	3.9%	Consumer Discretionary
Hasbro Inc	6.2%	Consumer Discretionary
Interpublic Group of Companies Inc	3.6%	Consumer Discretionary
Juniper Networks Inc	2.8%	Information

		Technology
Nordstrom Inc	3.7%	Consumer Discretionary
NCR Corp	6.2%	Information Technology
NVIDIA Corp	2.9%	Information Technology
Sabre Holdings Corp	6.8%	Information Technology
Unisys Corp	4.3%	Information Technology
Yum! Brands Inc	5.2%	Consumer Discretionary

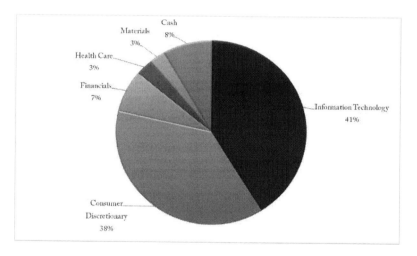

Figure 13-34 Initial Sector Allocation, 2007

By now we should be used to some fickle performance, after a few very mixed years. This year starts out quite well, moving up to +8% by late February. After that, we see a drop down below zero again, but it doesn't last long and it's not deep enough to trigger any scaling out. These things happen, nothing to worry about. That's the equity markets for you. We then start moving up, both fast and at a steady pace. Before the end of the summer, we're already up 17% on the year. Now that's quite a respectable performance, in particular since the index was just at +10% at the time.

From here, some volatility sets in and we see quite large moves in the portfolio. We're down to just a 3% gain on the year for a brief period before rallying up to +20%. The market is swinging quite a bit as well, but we can feel the heavy beta component here. Always be aware that a large part of equity momentum investing is about beta. We're likely to feel the swings in the index at a much higher magnitude than your average balanced portfolio.

The index is getting very close to the average and we're scaling exposure back and forth a bit over the year. Seeing another year where we're scaling out too early will surely lead many readers to think that the solution is to remove the index filter, or at least move it from a 200 day moving average to a 300 day equivalent. In chapter 14 you'll see why neither solution is a very good idea. For now, take my word for it.

Table 13-18 Results 2007

	Momentum Strategy	S&P 500 Total Return Index
Return 2007	17.3%	5.5%
Max Drawdown 2007	-12.8%	-9.9%
Annualized Return Since 1999	13.6%	3.7%
Max Drawdown since 1999	-18.5%	-47.4%

The exposure scaling throughout the year has certainly hurt performance, but we're still reaching the finish line in December with pretty good numbers. The index ended the year at +5.5% and we beat it with double digits. The momentum strategy finished at over +17% this year, proving its worth after the past tough year.

Figure 13-36 shows one of the more interesting trades of the year. We bought US Steel in January, rebalanced it a few times along the way and finally sold it after a slight pullback in July. An excellent trade and this is exactly what we want to see more of.

We had a decent year with both double digit performance and a welcome outperformance against the market. We've still got a bit of distance to cover to the high water mark we set in 2005, but we'll get there. Most importantly, we're showing a long term return profile that's significantly more attractive than passively buying and holding the index.

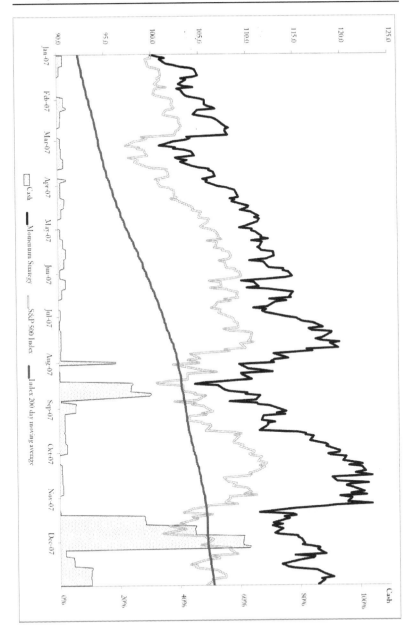

Figure 13-35 Performance, 2007

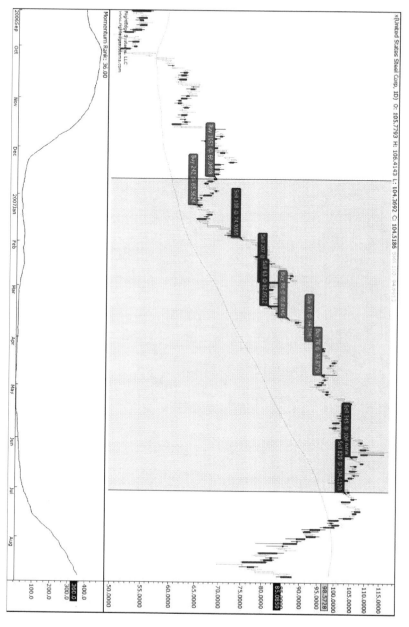

Figure 13-36 US Steel Corp

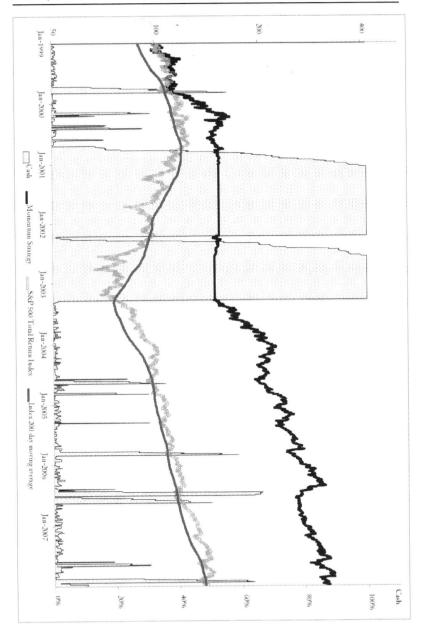

Figure 13-37 Performance 1999-2007

2008

If the number 2008 doesn't make you shiver and give you PTSD symptoms, you were probably lucky enough not to work in the business during this time. This was an incredibly stressful year. Even those few who came out of this year with strong performance still remember it with horror. Not that much time has passed but it's hard to think back to just how close to the edge we all were.

This was the year where the financial system nearly collapsed. Any bank could go bankrupt at any time. Most of us were shuffling around cash every day between banks, moving liquid assets to whatever bank seemed least likely to go under in the next 24 hours. Even though the market took an enormous hit this year, we were all lucky to get out of it at all.

Table 13-19 Initial Portfolio, 2008

Name	Weight	Sector
Apple Inc	2.7%	Information Technology
Assurant Inc	3.7%	Financials
Apache Corp	3.3%	Energy
Apollo Education Group Inc	2.6%	Consumer Discretionary
Peabody Energy Corp	2.6%	Energy
CONSOL Energy Inc	2.9%	Energy
Deere & Co	3.0%	Industrials
EOG Resources Inc	3.8%	Energy
Express Scripts Holding Co	4.0%	Health Care
Gilead Sciences Inc	3.3%	Health Care
Google Inc	3.2%	Information Technology
Jacobs Engineering Group Inc	2.9%	Industrials
McDonald's Corp	4.7%	Consumer Discretionary
Monsanto Co	2.8%	Materials
Murphy Oil Corp	3.7%	Energy
Newmont Mining Corp	2.7%	Materials

Northern Trust Corp	3.2% Financials
Occidental Petroleum Corp	3.0% Energy
The Pepsi Bottling Group Inc	3.8% Consumer Staples
Procter & Gamble Co	6.1% Consumer Staples
Transocean Ltd	3.0% Energy
Charles Schwab Corp	3.0% Financials
Molson Coors Brewing Co	3.4% Consumer Staples
Textron Inc	3.9% Industrials
Waters Corp	5.0% Health Care
Yum! Brands Inc	4.2% Consumer Discretionary

At the start of 2008, the index is already below the long term moving average. It dipped below just at the end of last year, and we had just started decreasing stocks a little bit. We have 10% of the portfolio in cash in January but when the market initially drops by about 10% in the first couple of weeks, we follow the index almost perfectly. Each week we sell a few stocks and as the index remains below the average, we're not replacing them. Note in Figure 13-39 how the cash slowly increases every week.

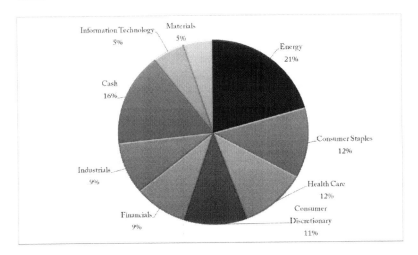

Figure 13-38 Initial Sector Allocation, 2008

Since we're quickly down to less than half exposure, and continuing to decrease from there, we don't see much portfolio movements from February on. In fact, by May we have absolutely zero exposure to the stock market remaining. We're all in cash.

As mentioned previously, it's important to remember that in such situations, cash doesn't mean leaving it on a bank account. Or even worse, leaving it in a brokerage account. Actual cash with a bank or broker is not safe. This cannot be stressed enough. If it wasn't clear to everyone before 2008, it sure was after. If your bank or broker has a problem, you can say good bye to your cash. You'll likely get securities back if your broker goes belly-up, but you'll never see that cash again. Anyone who thinks that this view is paranoid probably didn't experience 2008. Some of the most prestigious banks and brokers in the world blew up, taking the cash with them. Several more almost blew up but were saved in the last minute. Short term money market and similar safer hiding places are strongly recommended. When I use the word cash here, it's meant figuratively.

The thing about 2008 was that it started quite slow. From a long term perspective, we entered a bear market already from the start, but not much really happened from there. For several months, we saw a slow, sideways market with a bit of a negative tilt. Things didn't really start to look worrying until Bear Stearns took a dirt nap in March. Even after that, the markets seemed to start a slow recovery.

For an investor using a momentum approach with index trend filter, none of this mattered too much. Sure, it's still stressful just to watch the disturbing developments in the world, but it didn't have any impact on profits or losses. We were already in cash.

By late May, it may have seemed like a bad idea. After all, we're in cash and deadlocked at -8% until we get a green light to start buying again. The market on the other hand was back to +/-0% at that point. We're almost ten percent behind and all in cash. This can be more stressful than it may seem. It's one of those situations where it's very easy to override and start buying, in fear of falling behind.

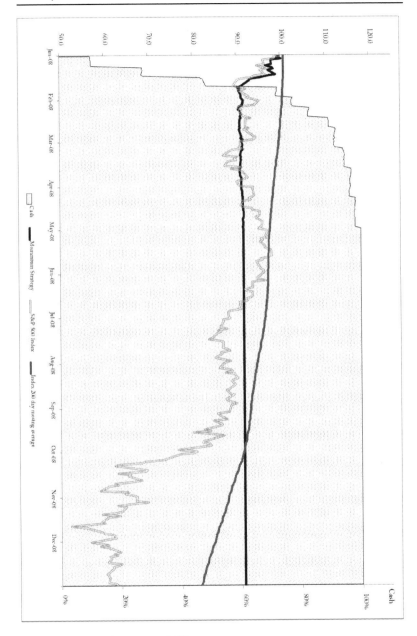

Figure 13-39 Performance, 2008

This is what the rules are here for. To guarantee consistent behavior over time. That's the only way that we can find some predictability in our returns.

Just a couple of months later, and now the index is back down below our flat lined performance. The index first went down to -15%, wobbled around for a couple of months, and then the real drama began.

The fall of '08 was like nothing we've ever seen before. If we're all very lucky, we'll never have to see anything like it again. The market went into free fall mode. Stocks were falling into a bottomless pit. At the start of October, we saw the S&P 500 having lost 40% on the year. This is the month when banks and brokers are blowing up left and right. There's nowhere to run, nowhere to hide.

In November, the S&P 500, the benchmark index for American large cap companies, is showing a loss of 47% since the start of the year. The American stock market has lost half of its value. In one year.

Our momentum portfolio? Oh, it's still anchored at -8%. The loss we took in January.

Sure, a loss of 8% isn't fun. But relative to almost everyone else, you're suddenly significantly better off, despite having made a loss.

Peabody Energy, in Figure 13-40, had its second failed trade in a row. We had a trade last year in this stock that failed right after it was initiated. In December 2007 it was bought again and even though it lasted for two months, it fell back pretty hard and caused some losses. This was far from the only stock showing this pattern early 2008. Many stocks were bought and held for only a couple of months before falling down and being closed with losses.

Consol Energy was one of the better stocks in 2008. This stock was also bought in December 2007 but it managed to survive remarkably long given the growing bear market. Consol was held all the way up to the end of April, when it was sold due to its rank briefly exceeding 100. After this stock was sold, we were all in cash.

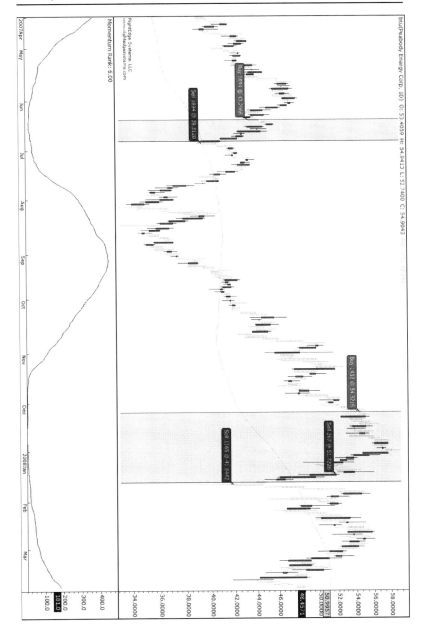

Figure 13-40 Peabody Energy

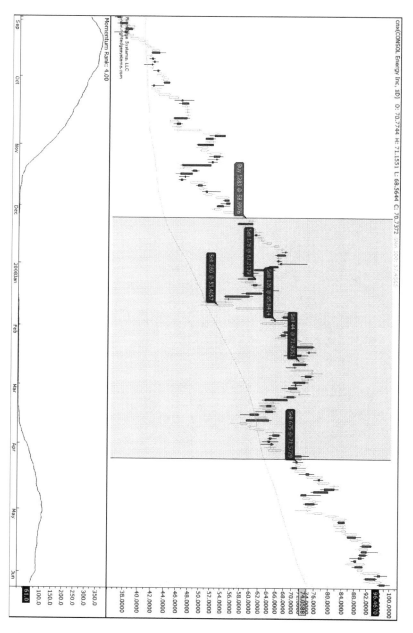

Figure 13-41 Consol Energy

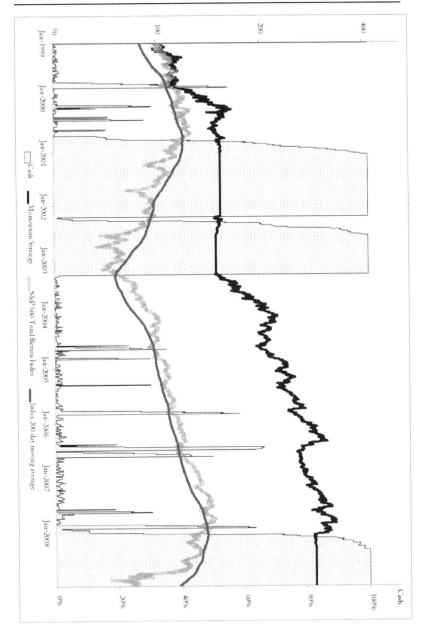

Figure 13-42 Performance 1999-2008

Remember how we went all flat-line back in 2001? We're back in that mode again. Now we've got a great long term track record and while the rest of the world is losing money by the minute, we're comfortable with just holding cash.

Table 13-20 Results 2008

	Momentum Strategy	S&P 500 Total Return Index
Return 2008	-8.5%	-37.0%
Max Drawdown 2008	-9.8%	-47.7%
Annualized Return Since 1999	11.2%	-1.4%
Max Drawdown since 1999	-18.5%	-50.7%

A buy and hold investor who invested $100 in the S&P 500 at the start of 1999 now has a loss of $15. Meanwhile, the same investment into the momentum strategy now shows a profit of $188 for the same time period.

2009

We really dodged the bullet on that one, huh? As the S&P 500 ended up losing 40% last year, we only dropped 10%. All this also means that the index is very far from the average. Predictably, we enter into 2009 without owning a single share. Early on in the year, this should have been a great relief to anyone trading this type of strategy. The 40% loss of last year wasn't enough. The S&P 500 index continued down after the holidays, falling first -14% in January and then continuing down to a massive 27% loss in March.

Today we know that this point, when we saw -27% in 2009, was the best point in a lifetime to buy stocks. It certainly didn't look like it at that time. It looked more like the world was about to fall apart. Granted that this is usually how the world looks just before a major bear market ends, but it simply wasn't predictable. You could just as easily have started buying a few months earlier. It wasn't an easy bottom to pick, and it's very rare that this is the case.

The markets made a sharp turn for the upside in March. Figure 13-43 shows how the index was miles away from the moving average at the time. The average kept moving down and the index kept moving up at steam engine speed. By June, the two are reintroduced after almost a year apart.

As the index crosses up over the average, we finally get a green light to start buying. Still, we only filled less than half of the portfolio. Any guess as to why?

Remember our buying criteria. Any stock with a recent move in excess of 15% is disqualified, as is any stock that's currently trading below its 100 day moving average. The last point is to make sure we don't become accidental bottom fishers. That rule also disqualified almost the entire S&P 500 membership at this point in time.

The qualifying stocks were ranked and we bought from the top of the list. Not until we ran out of cash, but until we ran out of stocks. It's an unusual situation, but it can happen.

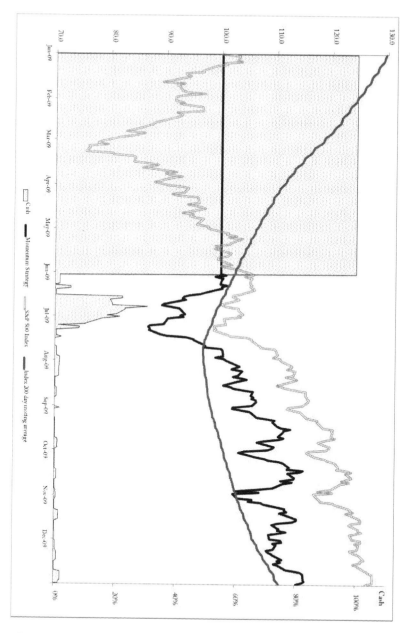

Figure 13-43 Performance, 2009

Table 13-21 Portfolio, June 2009

Name	Weight	Sector
Advanced Micro Devices Inc	1.4%	Information Technology
AutoNation Inc	1.8%	Consumer Discretionary
Allegheny Technologies Inc	1.7%	Materials
Big Lots Inc	1.8%	Consumer Discretionary
CF Industries Holdings Inc	2.5%	Materials
Ciena Corp	1.6%	Information Technology
CME Group Inc	2.1%	Financials
Coach Inc	1.9%	Consumer Discretionary
Goldman Sachs Group Inc	2.5%	Financials
Goodyear Tire & Rubber Co	1.2%	Consumer Discretionary
Starwood Hotels & Resorts Worldwide Inc	1.7%	Consumer Discretionary
Intercontinental Exchange Inc	2.3%	Financials
Interpublic Group of Companies Inc	1.7%	Consumer Discretionary
Johnson Controls Inc	2.0%	Consumer Discretionary
J C Penney Company Inc	1.6%	Consumer Discretionary
Meredith Corp	2.4%	Consumer Discretionary
Motorola Solutions Inc	2.0%	Information Technology
Monster Worldwide Inc	1.6%	Information Technology
Nabors Industries Ltd	1.7%	Energy
Pioneer Natural Resources Co	1.6%	Energy
Sealed Air Corp	2.5%	Materials

The initial portfolio bought can be seen in Table 13-21. It's a diverse mix of sectors with no clear theme. An overweight in discretionary, but nothing remarkable. These are simply the stocks that recovered quickest. The ones that weren't disqualified by being below their moving averages.

In the beginning, just after this portfolio was constructed, things got a little volatile. That's normal and it's always a little nervous when you start buying again after a significant bear market. We're not trying to time the exact bottom here. Such methods almost always fail in reality anyhow. We just want back in when it's reasonable to expect that the bear market may have ended.

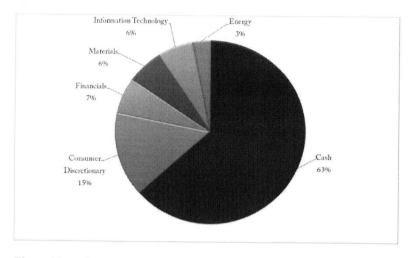

Figure 13-44 Sector Allocation, June 2009

In the first couple of months, our new portfolio loses 7%, which was slightly more than the index. After that however, things are looking better. For the rest of the year, we keep moving up. What we got was an underperformance against the benchmark index, mostly because we scaled in slowly and didn't participate fully until September. Still, we did manage to cash in on double digit returns in a difficult year. The index ended up gaining over 26% while we reached 14%.

The Franklin trade in Figure 13-45 made a welcome contribution to the performance this year. It was bought in July and started rallying right after. The volatility was quite erratic, resulting in many rebalancing trades before the position was closed with a nice profit in December.

Table 13-22 Results 2009

	Momentum Strategy	S&P 500 Total Return Index
Return 2009	14.0%	26.5%
Max Drawdown 2009	-14.1%	-27.2%
Annualized Return Since 1999	11.4%	0.9%
Max Drawdown since 1999	-24.3%	-55.3%

On the whole, we're finally back. After a year out of the market, we went all in and just made a new all-time high. While we missed part of the market recovery, our strategy was never designed to capture V-shape turnarounds. The momentum strategy handled the bear market well and our outperformance in the long run is substantial.

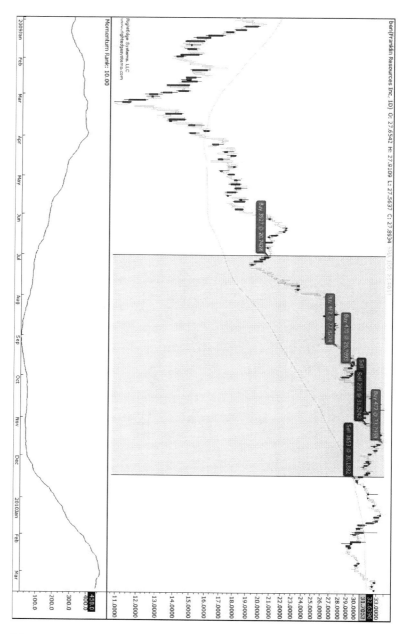

Figure 13-45 Franklin Resources

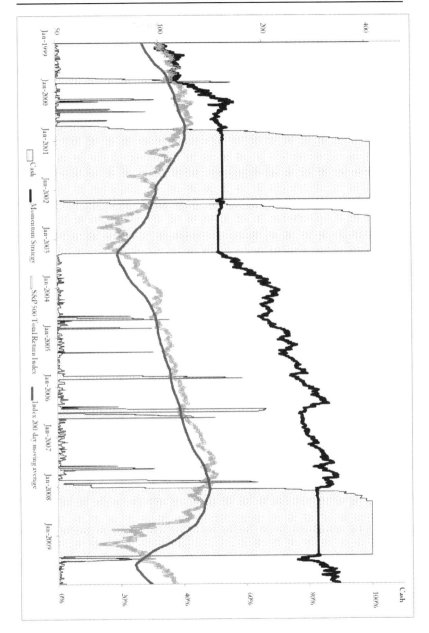

Figure 13-46 Performance 1999-2009

2010

What we need to be really happy with this strategy is a prolonged bull market. A sideways market doesn't hurt that much, but it won't gain too much either. Unfortunately, 2010 isn't the year of the ultimate bull market.

We start off with a portfolio heavy in IT and discretionary, with a dash of health care and materials. You may have noticed the pattern now, that tech and discretionary tend to be overrepresented in momentum portfolios. This is not by design, but merely due to the fact that these stocks generally show higher momentum, or at least did in the recent decades.

Table 13-23 Initial Portfolio, 2010

Name	Weight	Sector
Akamai Technologies Inc	2.9%	Information Technology
Ameriprise Financial Inc	3.4%	Financials
Cardinal Health Inc	6.2%	Health Care
Caterpillar Inc	3.4%	Industrials
Cliffs Natural Resources Inc	2.6%	Materials
Salesforce.com Inc	3.4%	Information Technology
Cognizant Technology Solutions Corp	4.6%	Information Technology
Estee Lauder Companies Inc	4.0%	Consumer Staples
Freeport-McMoRan Inc	3.1%	Materials
FLIR Systems Inc	4.3%	Information Technology
Google Inc	7.9%	Information Technology
Harman International Industries Inc	2.5%	Consumer Discretionary
Harris Corp	5.1%	Information Technology
Jabil Circuit Inc	2.8%	Information Technology
Nordstrom Inc	3.5%	Consumer Discretionary

Lexmark International Inc	3.3% Information Technology
Alpha Appalachia Holdings Inc	2.7% Energy
MeadWestvaco Corp	3.7% Materials
Mylan Inc	4.4% Health Care
NetApp Inc	3.9% Information Technology
PNC Financial Services Group Inc	3.2% Financials
Pioneer Natural Resources Co	3.0% Energy
RadioShack Corp	3.2% Consumer Discretionary
Tiffany & Co	3.1% Consumer Discretionary
Whirlpool Corp	3.8% Consumer Discretionary
Wyndham Worldwide Corp	3.1% Consumer Discretionary

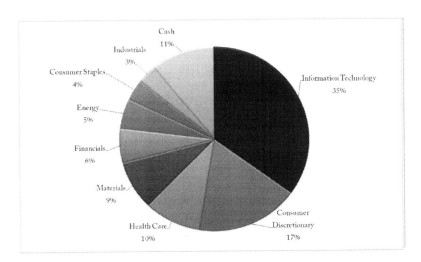

Figure 13-47 Initial Sector Allocation, 2010

We had an initial drop in portfolio value early in the year, which was almost exactly in-line with what the index did. Up until early March, the strategy tracked the index remarkably well. At that point, the strategy took off and the index quickly fell behind. By May, we had gains of 19% on the year while the index didn't even reach double digits.

That was also our best reading of what turned out to be a rather turbulent year. From nearly 20 percent up, we fell right back down, losing it all and then some. The index fell too, but we fell harder. At the lows in August, we were at -7% since the start of the year and right back next to the index.

The index itself spent much of the summer under the average and that resulted in our strategy scaling exposure up and down a few times as the index wobbled around the average. When the index drops down below the average, one of two things usually happens. Either the market goes into bear mode, leaving us to keep slowly scaling out, seeing smaller losses while the index loses much more, or the index comes right back up again and we struggle to keep up. The latter is much more common and that's an acceptable price to pay for the downside protection that we get.

This is what happens in this case. The market moves right back up and as we're on low exposure we miss out on much of the initial advance. While we recover and keep moving up for the rest of the year, we don't manage to catch up to the index before the end of December. Well, we still ended with a near 12% gain on the year, so it's not bad. This is a long term strategy and in the long run we're both strongly positive and very far ahead of the benchmark index.

Sandisk was a nice trade in 2010, even though it ended with a gap down. Shown in Figure 13-49, the stock was held for the better part of the year. Biogen, in Figure 13-50 was less fun however. It was one of many stocks that took a hit early in the year, causing the large give-back of performance as the overall market dropped.

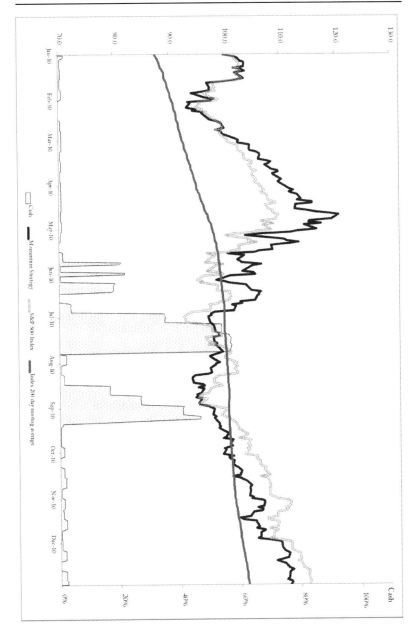

Figure 13-48 Performance, 2010

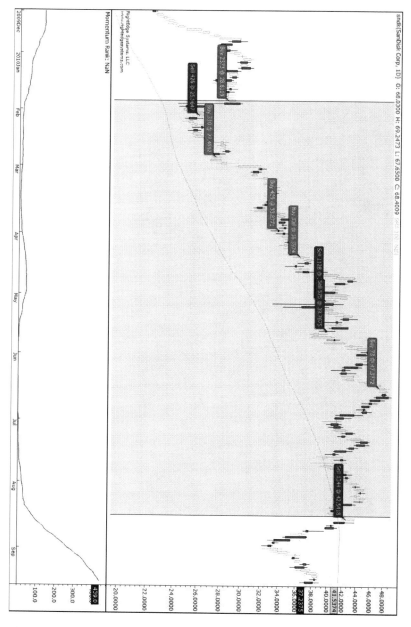

Figure 13-49 Sandisk

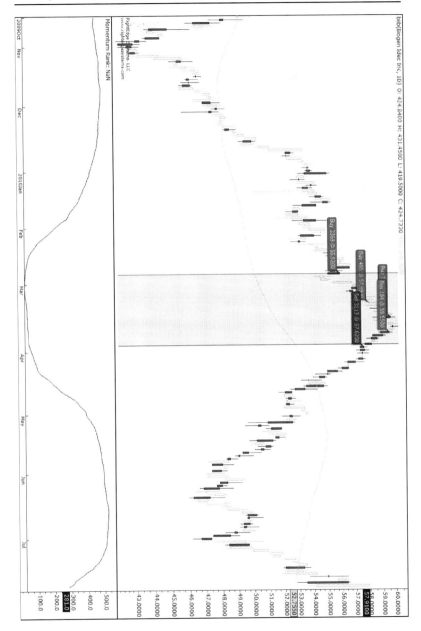

Figure 13-50 Biogen Idec

Table 13-24 Results 2010

	Momentum Strategy	S&P 500 Total Return Index
Return 2010	11.7%	15.1%
Max Drawdown 2010	-22.1%	-15.6%
Annualized Return Since 1999	11.4%	2.0%
Max Drawdown since 1999	-24.3%	-55.3%

We made a significant new high and then backed off from it. This is quite common and to be expected. Unfortunately, it's not easy to time these things. Consistency tends to win in the long run, not market timing.

Figure 13-51 shows just how far ahead of the market we are at this point. What might appear in many years to be a small outperformance really adds up in the long run. The stable players tend to last.

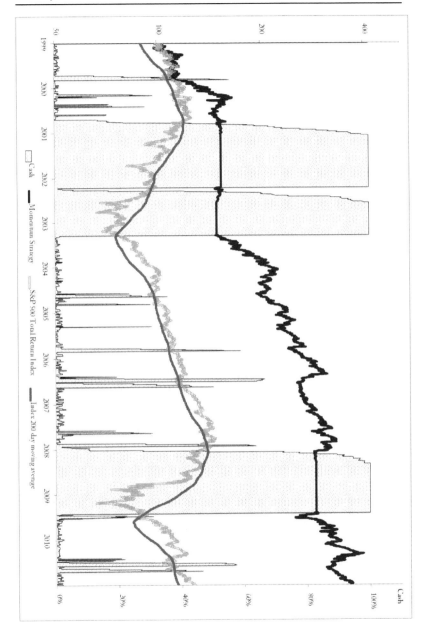

Figure 13-51 Performance 1999-2010

2011

Isn't it great how we never really had a bad year? We did lose money in 2008 of course, but in the context of the index massacre, our loss wasn't really much to worry about. We never had a year where we experienced a significant loss and at the same time underperform the index. Well, that's all about to change.

We go into 2011 holding a large amount of discretionary stocks, with energy and tech having significant exposure. While the market seemed perfectly stable at this time, we're in for a bumpy ride. Buckle up and brace for impact.

Table 13-25 Initial Portfolio, 2011

Name	Weight	Sector
Amazon.com Inc	4.3%	Consumer Discretionary
Abercrombie & Fitch Co	3.5%	Consumer Discretionary
Anadarko Petroleum Corp	4.2%	Energy
Beam Suntory Inc	4.6%	Consumer Staples
CF Industries Holdings Inc	3.0%	Materials
Coach Inc	4.4%	Consumer Discretionary
Compuware Corp	4.1%	Information Technology
Freeport-McMoRan Inc	3.5%	Materials
Harman International Industries Inc	3.9%	Consumer Discretionary
Hess Corp	4.4%	Energy
Johnson Controls Inc	4.6%	Consumer Discretionary
J C Penney Company Inc	3.3%	Consumer Discretionary
Juniper Networks Inc	4.1%	Information Technology
Carmax Inc	3.2%	Consumer Discretionary
L Brands Inc	3.9%	Consumer Discretionary
LSI Corp	3.6%	Information Technology
Alpha Appalachia Holdings Inc	3.4%	Energy
National Oilwell Varco Inc	3.6%	Energy
NVIDIA Corp	3.4%	Information Technology
Pioneer Natural Resources Co	4.6%	Energy

Red Hat Inc	3.7% Information Technology
Schlumberger NV	4.6% Energy
Tiffany & Co	4.5% Consumer Discretionary
T-Mobile US Inc	3.7% Telecommunication Services
Western Digital Corp	3.8% Information Technology

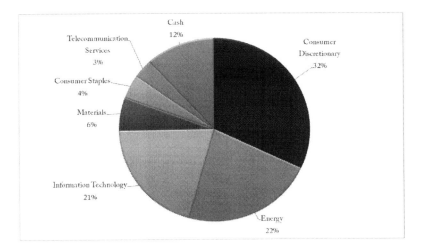

Figure 13-52 Initial Sector Allocation, 2011

The performance starts out quite choppy, and it's about to get worse. For the first part of the year, we see a yo-yo like performance, moving between 5-6 percent up and down several times. During this period, the moving average keeps creeping closer and closer to the index. Then in August, we saw something big.

The combination of a sovereign debt crisis in Europe and a downgrade of the US credit rating can be a bit of a drag on the stock markets. The big hit came in August, when the S&P 500 Index lost nearly 20% in a two week window. That's quite a dramatic move and it came out of the blue. There was no slow trend reversal or other common signs of a market turn. We had an orderly sideways market within a larger bull market, and suddenly this happens.

In a situation like this, momentum players tend to get hit hard. Having a portfolio fully loaded with high beta stocks in a sudden market plunge is not a fun experience. In this case, almost surprisingly, our strategy only took about the same damage as the index, and even slightly less in the initial phase.

Before this event, we had been moving between +8% and -3%. As the market suddenly went on an unscheduled southbound expedition, we were at more or less zero for the year. Within two weeks we found ourselves in a 12% hole and in the process of scaling out stocks. Each week, several stocks were sold in the regular rebalancing and as the index dropped far below the average, we're not allowed to replace them. The cash is building up fast and in just a few more weeks we're almost entirely out of the stock markets.

What happened next is annoying but it's the cost of the downside protection that a trend filter offers. Our trend filter has made sure that we're now scaled out of the market. This was exactly when the market recovered again. Poor timing, once again. Well, this is a long term approach and in the long run a protection mechanism like this trend filter can greatly improve performance, despite causing the occasional headache.

Table 13-26 Results 2011

	Momentum Strategy	S&P 500 Total Return Index
Return 2011	-9.3%	2.1%
Max Drawdown 2011	-21.1%	-18.6%
Annualized Return Since 1999	9.7%	2.0%
Max Drawdown since 1999	-24.3%	-55.3%

The market bounced back and ended nearly marginally positive, while our strategy stayed firmly anchored down at almost -10%.

Sprint, in Figure 13-54, shows one of many bad trades in 2011. We bought the stock in late June after a strong first half year. As it turned out, this was the worst possible time to buy the stock. It fell right back down and went into a choppy sideways phase until finally kicking us out at the lows. All in all a horribly frustrating trade, but this is all part of the game.

A very similar situation is shown in Figure 13-55, where we had another bad trade in O'Reilly Automotive. This was even more frustrating in that it took off on the upside, showing a great rally just after we exited.

Well, so we gave back some performance. We're still doing pretty well in the long run. The downside protection is in place and once the markets stabilize we'll probably do well again.

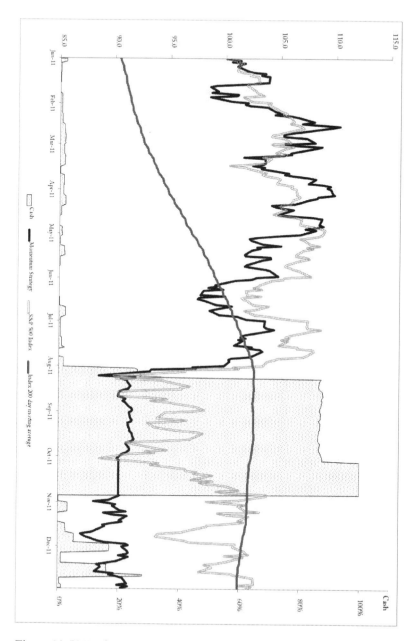

Figure 13-53 Performance, 2011

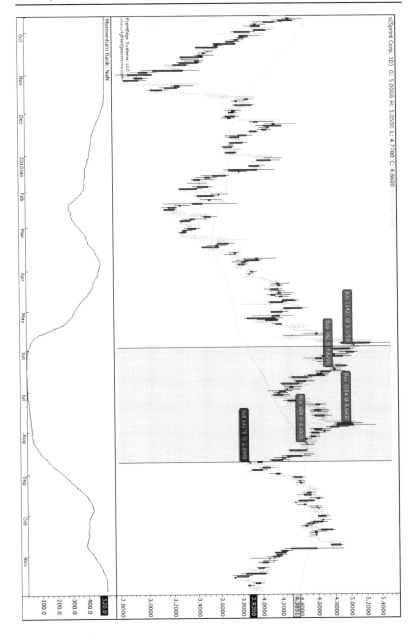

Figure 13-54 Sprint

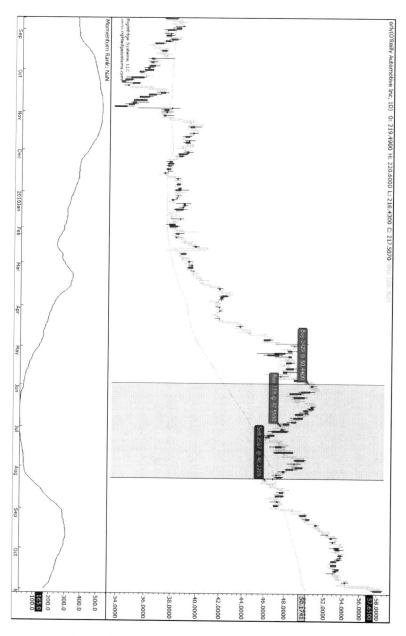

Figure 13-55 O'Reilly Automotive

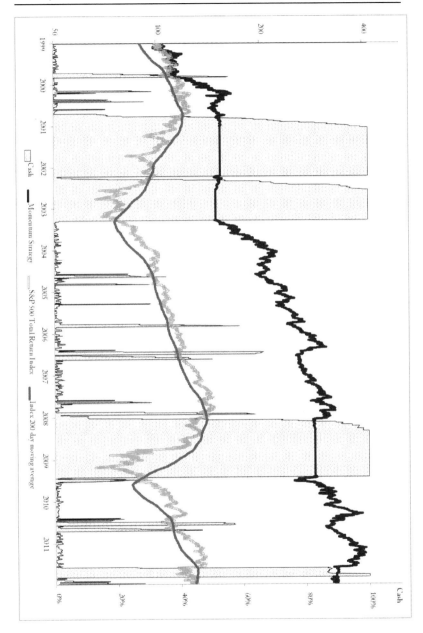

Figure 13-56 Performance 1999-2011

2012

We enter 2012 with a full portfolio, having just bought back in December last year. We're heavy in discretionary with some additions of industrials, tech and a few scattered allocations to other sectors. Compared to the previous few years, we've got a very low allocation to the tech sector. Performance of sectors tends to vary greatly and lately the tech sector didn't do well enough to get the same over-allocation as prior years. Remember that we don't use any sector constraints at all here. The top stocks are bought, regardless of sector belonging and the overall sector composition can land anywhere it wants to.

Table 13-27 Initial Portfolio, 2012

Name	Weight	Sector
Beam Suntory Inc	5.0%	Consumer Staples
Big Lots Inc	3.0%	Consumer Discretionary
Biogen Idec Inc	4.2%	Health Care
Cisco Systems Inc	3.3%	Information Technology
Dean Foods Co	3.5%	Consumer Staples
D.R. Horton Inc	2.6%	Consumer Discretionary
Fastenal Co	4.2%	Industrials
F5 Networks Inc	2.4%	Information Technology
Goodrich Corp	11.7%	Industrials
W W Grainger Inc	4.2%	Industrials
Host Hotels & Resorts Inc	3.0%	Financials
Intuitive Surgical Inc	3.9%	Health Care
Jabil Circuit Inc	2.5%	Information Technology
J C Penney Company Inc	3.1%	Consumer Discretionary
KLA-Tencor Corp	2.9%	Information Technology
Lennar Corp	2.7%	Consumer Discretionary
Lowe's Companies Inc	3.8%	Consumer

		Discretionary
Macy's Inc	3.1%	Consumer Discretionary
Novellus Systems Inc	2.4%	Information Technology
ONEOK Inc	5.4%	Energy
O'Reilly Automotive Inc	4.7%	Consumer Discretionary
PulteGroup Inc	1.9%	Consumer Discretionary
Rockwell Automation Inc	2.8%	Industrials
Ross Stores Inc	4.4%	Consumer Discretionary
SanDisk Corp	2.5%	Information Technology
TJX Companies Inc	5.2%	Consumer Discretionary

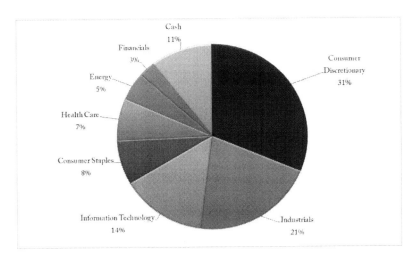

Figure 13-57 Initial Sector Allocation, 2012

2012 was a bit of a roller coaster year. It's one of those years where you've had times when you've been very happy, tearing your hair in frustration and then go back to being very happy again. Since we ended last year on a bad note, at least it's comforting to see an initial rally here. Our profits quickly add up as we've got a very strong portfolio of momentum stocks.

The portfolio rallies from day one and keeps on going until late March. At that time, we have a profit of 17%.

Having a large gain early in the year feels great, but always keep in mind that we're in this for the long run. Anything can happen. It can double or it can all go away. Try to avoid falling into the trap of calculating what 17% per quarter would mean for the whole year. Yes, it's tough not to do his math. In fact, I already did it for you. It's 87.4%. Of course we're not going to end up with a gain of 87.4%.

After having held that gain of 17%, the market takes a turn onto the southbound lane and we're coming along for the ride. Here our momentum stocks reacted rather predictably, in that the high beta component made us feel the drop much more than what the overall market felt. Our +17% profit is quickly reduced to -0.5% by May.

These situations are horribly frustrating. Whenever this happens, you'll hear someone trying to convince you that you should trade some magical forex signal system instead and gain thousands of pips per day. Ignore those people. Don't even ask what a pip is.

These dips are the cost of doing business. They happen and that's fine. If you manage to compound in the low double digits over longer periods of time, you'll beat most people out there. Even those with the magical pips generating super signals. They will have blown up all their accounts a long time ago.

From May on, things get a bit more fun. This was the bottom of the year and we start moving back up again. We're alternating between leading and lagging the index for a while, but after a choppy fall we have a strong finish of the year and end up beating the market with a very respectable return of 19%.

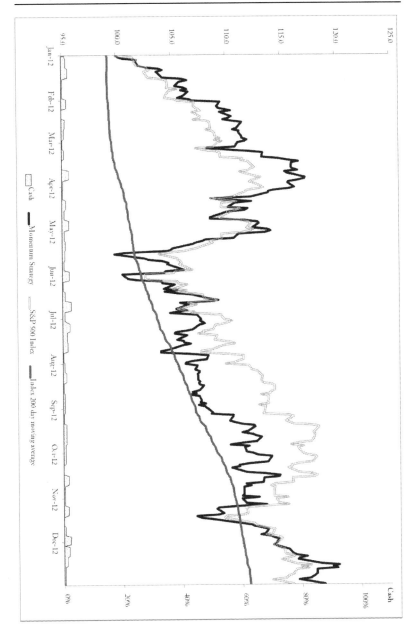

Figure 13-58 Performance, 2012

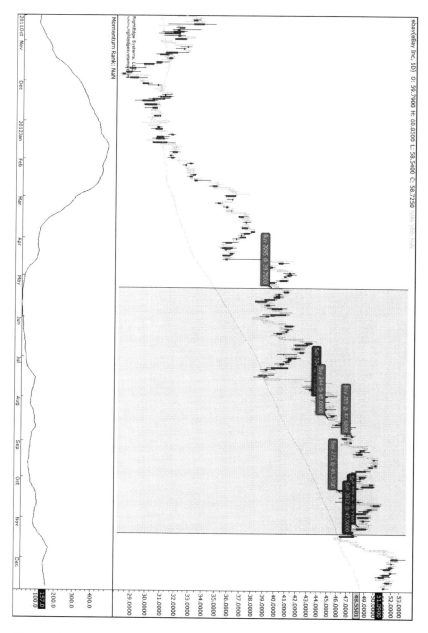

Figure 13-59 eBay

One of many great positions during 2012 was eBay, shown in Figure 13-59. The stock just kept going up the whole time. So why, might you ask, did we sell it if it just kept going up? Well, in a bull market, there are plenty of stocks that go up. We've now entered a new bull phase and that means that there are plenty of stocks to choose from. The trick is in having the right ones.

Table 13-28 Results 2012

	Momentum Strategy	S&P 500 Total Return Index
Return 2012	18.9%	16.0%
Max Drawdown 2012	-14.9%	-9.6%
Annualized Return Since 1999	10.3%	2.9%
Max Drawdown since 1999	-24.3%	-55.3%

While eBay may keep moving up, at one point it moved down the ranking list so far that it was no longer in the top 100 stocks in the index. That means that we sell it and buy something from the top of the list. If we don't have such a rule in place, we may end up holding sub-standard stocks just because they move up. In a bull market, it's not a merit to move up. Almost all stocks do that. We want the best.

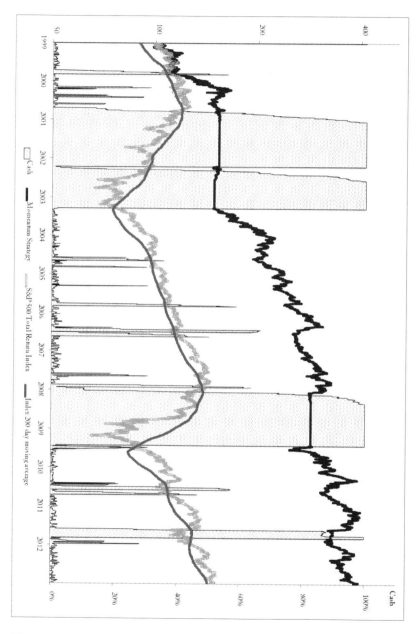

Figure 13-60 Performance 1999-2012

2013

In early 2013 there's little doubt that we're in a bull market. The usual suits on various market TV shows are taking turns explaining why the bull market is about to end. The common explanations have to do with excessive money printing, artificial buying pressure fueled by central bank policies and such. None of this really matters to us as momentum players. What matters is that the market is moving up and we're joining it. When it stops, we know that we have a safeguard in place to take us out of it. There's no reason to second guess the market. Why it's moving up really doesn't matter. Trying to pick tops will almost always fail.

As we enter into 2013, we still have a large allocation of discretionary stocks. More interestingly though, we now have a substantial holding of financial stocks. The ongoing quantitative easing programs have greatly helped this sector and the stocks are heading north faster than Santa on December 26.

Table 13-29 Initial Portfolio, 2013

Name	Weight	Sector
Bank of America Corp	3.7%	Financials
Peabody Energy Corp	1.9%	Energy
Citigroup Inc	3.7%	Financials
Cigna Corp	5.0%	Health Care
Computer Sciences Corp	4.2%	Information Technology
Gilead Sciences Inc	3.8%	Health Care
GameStop Corp	3.4%	Consumer Discretionary
Genworth Financial Inc	3.3%	Financials
Hudson City Bancorp Inc	4.1%	Financials
Hartford Financial Services Group Inc	4.8%	Financials
Leggett & Platt Inc	5.0%	Consumer Discretionary
Lennar Corp	3.3%	Consumer Discretionary
Lowe's Companies Inc	4.0%	Consumer Discretionary
Moody's Corp	5.4%	Financials

Marathon Petroleum Corp	3.7% Energy
M&T Bank Corp	6.4% Financials
Netflix Inc	2.1% Consumer Discretionary
Newell Rubbermaid Inc	6.4% Consumer Discretionary
PulteGroup Inc	2.4% Consumer Discretionary
Tenet Healthcare Corp	3.9% Health Care
Tyson Foods Inc	5.6% Consumer Staples
Whirlpool Corp	3.6% Consumer Discretionary
Wynn Resorts Ltd	4.3% Consumer Discretionary
Yahoo! Inc	5.5% Information Technology

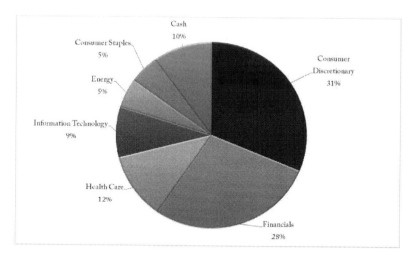

Figure 13-61 Initial Sector Allocation, 2013

Even though we had a respectable performance last year, it was still a bumpy ride. Don't you wish you could have at least one year with great performance, without any pesky little potholes along the way? Well, you're in luck. Just relax and enjoy the ride. We've got this.

The market started moving up slowly early on, but we didn't. We moved up fast. In February, we already had double digit gains. Queue compound math calculations.

You've probably noticed in earlier years how there were several times when we had strong gains early in the year, only to give it all away soon after. Perhaps you've been wondering if it wouldn't be a good idea to simply take the sign down and go home when a certain target is hit. After all, this year we've hit +15% in early March. Why not cash out and go fishing for the rest of the year?

This is the year that should teach you why fishing can be more expensive than you may think. See, this year just kept going. There were a few ups and downs, but in retrospect there're barely visible. The +15% in March turned into only +7% by May, but then it just kept on going and going, like a little Energizer bunny.

Most of the year we keep an even footing with the index. Over a period of multiple years, it would sound pretty mediocre if you're only showing index level performance. This year however, no one complained about getting the index.

For the whole year, pundits were competing in the art of calling a top. Everybody wants to be remembered as the guy who predicted the end. The problem is that no one will remember when you were wrong, only the one time that you were finally right. In the end, the proverbial stopped clock will become a market guru for his accurate prediction.

Ignore all these predictions about the end of a bull market. The most likely thing to happen in a bull market is for the bull market to continue. Just let it ride, and let an automatic market trend filter ease you out when the time comes.

This year ended with a massive return of over 37 percent. That's an extremely high return in the stock markets. Don't expect that to happen very often.

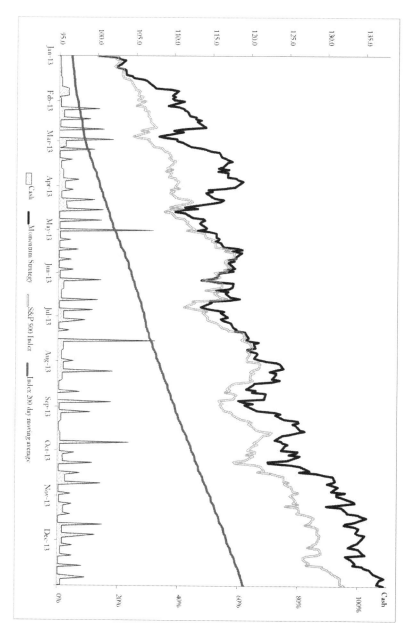

Figure 13-62 Performance, 2013

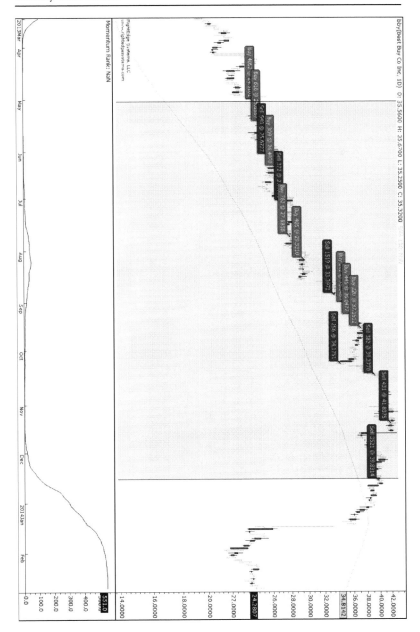

Figure 13-63 Best Buy

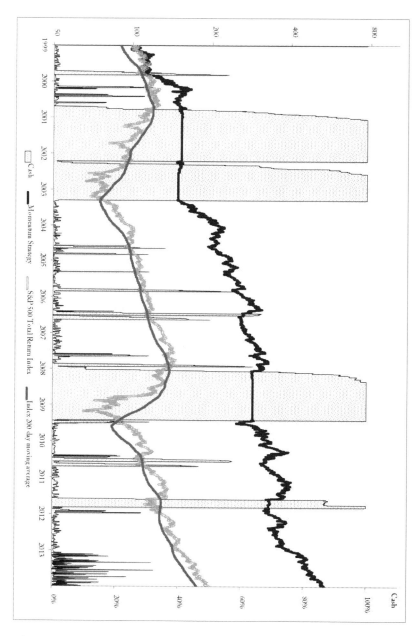

Figure 13-64 Performance 1999-2013

Things are fun in a bull market. The term Target Rich Environment comes to mind. In a strong bull market, we get a large amount of stocks that just take off and keep moving up. Best buy, in Figure 13-63, was one of them. We held this stock for almost the whole year.

Table 13-30 Results 2013

	Momentum Strategy	S&P 500 Total Return Index
Return 2013	37.5%	32.4%
Max Drawdown 2013	-7.4%	-5.6%
Annualized Return Since 1999	11.9%	4.7%
Max Drawdown since 1999	-24.3%	-55.3%

After some extremely good performance, an initial $100 in the momentum strategy is now worth over $500. The recovery in the overall market since the bottom in 2008 has been strong, but nothing compared to what a momentum strategy could do in the same time period.

2014

Having come from such a strong bull run, the confidence in the approach should be high at this time. We've seen very strong absolute returns last year, but we also saw a performance very close to the overall index. It would be nice to see both strong absolute returns and a significant outperformance in the same year.

Table 13-31 Initial Portfolio, 2014

Name	Weight	Sector
Amazon.com Inc	5.0%	Consumer Discretionary
Chipotle Mexican Grill Inc	6.2%	Consumer Discretionary
Cognizant Technology Solutions Corp	6.5%	Information Technology
Delta Air Lines Inc	3.7%	Industrials
E*TRADE Financial Corp	5.1%	Financials
Expedia Inc	4.0%	Consumer Discretionary
First Solar Inc	2.3%	Information Technology
Gilead Sciences Inc	3.8%	Health Care
Harman International Industries Inc	4.0%	Consumer Discretionary
Southwest Airlines Co	4.5%	Industrials
McKesson Corp	6.2%	Health Care
Micron Technology Inc	2.9%	Information Technology
Northrop Grumman Corp	7.2%	Industrials
Pitney Bowes Inc	3.9%	Industrials
Constellation Brands Inc	7.2%	Consumer Staples
Safeway Inc	3.6%	Consumer Staples
Valero Energy Corp	4.2%	Energy
Wynn Resorts Ltd	5.0%	Consumer Discretionary
United States Steel Corp	3.5%	Materials
Xylem Inc	5.5%	Industrials
Yahoo! Inc	4.4%	Information Technology

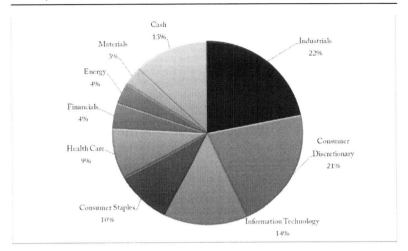

Figure 13-65 Initial Sector Allocation, 2014

2014 was an overall fun year to be in momentum stocks. There was one event that felt very worrying at the time, but which was quickly forgotten. To start out with, we saw a very nice initial push, giving us a head start on the index of 5% in the first few days. This is a very comfortable spot to start the year, and in particular as the market saw a drop of about the same magnitude in February. The market dropped 5% and we shaved off the same. While the market was left at -5% on the year, we're at about zero. From there, it was mostly a big rally for half a year. There was some volatility along the way, but nothing really worrying in any way.

Table 13-32 Results 2014

	Momentum Strategy	S&P 500 Total Return Index
Return 2014	18.4%	13.7%
Max Drawdown 2014	-10.7%	-7.3%
Annualized Return Since 1999	12.3%	5.2%
Max Drawdown since 1999	-24.3%	-55.3%

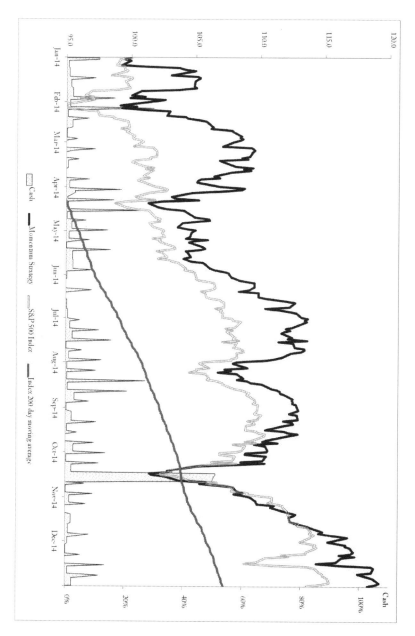

Figure 13-66 Performance, 2014

The worrying event came around in October. The index suddenly moved down rapidly. While no one could be bothered to remember why a few months later, at the time the headlines were talking about fear of an end Quantitative Easing, slowing European growth and other factors that really shouldn't have been a major surprise to anyone.

The market turned down hard and our momentum stocks ended up losing significantly more than the market. Having seen gains of over 17% on the year, we're now suddenly back to +5% in just a few days. At this time, the index is below the average again and we start scaling out of stocks.

Once again, we started scaling out at a very bad time. This market scare was very temporary, and before the month was over, the index was back above where it started. We were initially left behind with a low exposure, but that's when our stocks really took off.

From that point, we went on a rampage with an end of year rally that took us all the way to +24%. That's a very strong year and it also means that we beat the market by a wide margin. The S&P 500 landed at around +14%, giving us a 10% lead.

Allergan, in Figure 13-67, was an interesting trade this year. It was bought in February after having had a very strong run up for a few months. In late March it was almost sold when it dipped down and started falling in the ranking list. Then suddenly, the stock made a 25% advance in a matter of days, making an already profitable position into one of the big winners of the year. After this however, it kept moving sideways for several months. We didn't sell it, because it was still highly ranked. When it finally dropped down a bit again in late summer, it was sold with a very healthy profit.

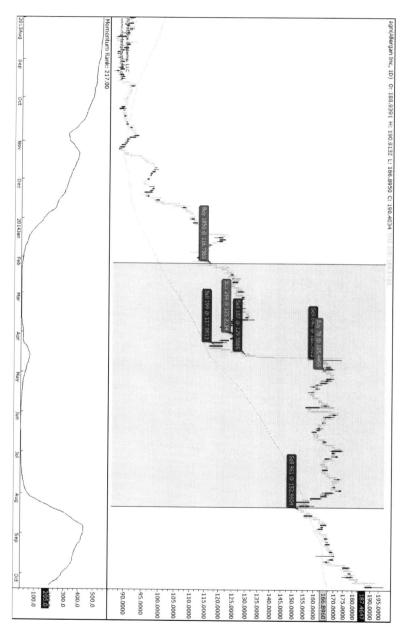

Figure 13-67 Allergan

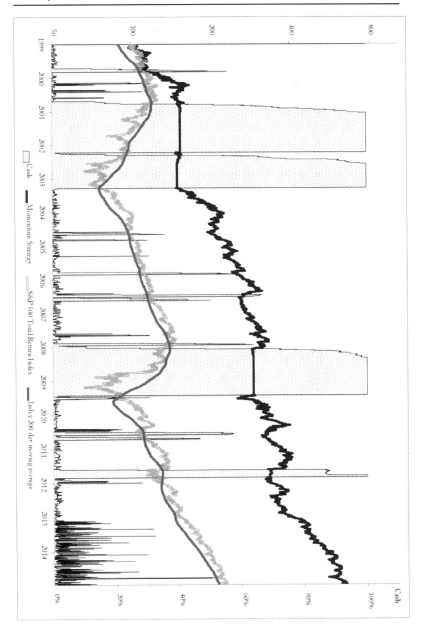

Figure 13-68 Performance 1999-2014

Conclusions of Year by Year Review

Making a good looking simulation isn't all that difficult. It's when you actually deploy it when the real problems start. When you look at a long term simulation chart or a monthly table of results, things seem very easy. It's not difficult to take the long term perspective when you're faced with such data. When you're right in the middle of it though, it's a whole different game.

The irony is that many people who deploy solid long term strategies quickly succumb to the short term stress and start changing their models. If you launch a long term strategy without being fully aware of what type of behavior to expect from it, you're not very likely to stick to it.

What I wanted to show you in this chapter was just how difficult and frustrating it can be in the short run. Once you're sitting there with big money at risk and the market's moving fast against you, it's a whole other world. It helps to do all the simulation work, so that you know that the strategy would have worked in the past. That gives some comfort and helps you to stick to the rules during the bad periods. It's not enough of course.

Nothing can properly prepare you for live deployment of a trading model. If you're lucky, you launch at the right time by pure accident and your returns are great from the start. If you get a couple of good years to start off with, it's easier to stick to the rules during the bad years. If you happen to start off with a bad year though, it's very easy to throw in the towel.

Hopefully this chapter has helped somewhat to prepare you for the ups and downs of managing a momentum investment strategy. Still, there's only one real test. The only way to know if you can do it or not, is to try it with real money.

14
Strategy Analysis

What we've seen so far is a fully working momentum investment model. The results over time are strong and it has stood the test of time. Bull or bear market, this model has shown great outperformance over time. The rules should now be clear and they were presented in detail in chapter 10. They work quite well the way that they have been presented but a strategy that requires an exact set of rules to work is usually not a very robust strategy. The question then is which of these rules are critical and which ones are not. This chapter will look at the different components of the strategy to see if and how they can be changed. If you understand what's important and what's not, it will help you understand the logic behind the rules and how the money is made.

How important is the Trend Filter?

As you've no doubt have noticed in chapter 13, the trend filter can be quite annoying at times. Many times, it has made us scale down exposure just when we were close to the bottom. The market rallied after, and we were left behind. It's only natural to question the need for such a trend filter in the first place. After all, there were only two periods in 15 years where we really got any significant value from having this trend filter.

The short answer is that a trend filter adds plenty of value. It's there to make sure that you don't go down with the ship when the market really turns down. And it will really turn down, sooner or later, rest assured. The money saved during the long bear markets makes a huge difference in the long run.

If you're not convinced about the value of an index level trend filter, let's do a quick test to settle that question. The lines in Figure 14-1 speaks for itself. It's the exact same trading rules as we've used so far, but disregarding the index trend. That means that we're always in the market, always replacing stocks as they go out. We buy as long as there are any stocks out there that fulfill our criteria. We still have some scaling down in bear markets, as there eventually will be very few stocks in the index that can pass our filters. Note how there's some difference in the returns during the 2000-2003 bear market. After that, the strategy performs the same with or without the index filter, up until 2008. Here our filterless strategy takes a hit of over 50%. We suddenly lost half of our money in a short period of time.

Sure, the market also lost about half, but that's beside the point. Taking such a big hit means that you're too far behind to ever catch up again. We still end up beating the benchmark index without the trend filter, but we'll never catch up to those who filtered out the bear markets.

If you looked at those long term simulation results earlier and wondered about the long flat periods, it should now be a bit clearer. With our momentum strategy, we had two long periods without any gains. The return was absolutely flat for a long time, even years in the case of the 2000-2003 markets. What's important to remember is that these were horrible times to trade stocks. Almost everyone lost, and they lost big.

After the fact, people tend to say that you should have been short. Most people saying that didn't really trade though those periods. Fact of the matter is that most people trading the short side in a strong bear market, end up losing money. The short side is extremely difficult and those who say otherwise tend to be people who lack actual experience on the subject.

But the question on the poor timing remains. We had many false signals in our strategy. Many times did the index dive down under the 200 day moving average, only to rally right back up after we started scaling out. Couldn't we optimize this?

No, we can't. Optimizations are evil and out to kill you. Don't trust them.

For this book, I picked settings almost randomly. I picked numbers that made sense with absolutely no optimization. I didn't run any simulations first to make sure that the numbers were the best possible. That would just be silly. It would just make the results look unrealistically good. It wouldn't help anyone. Except perhaps sell a few more books.

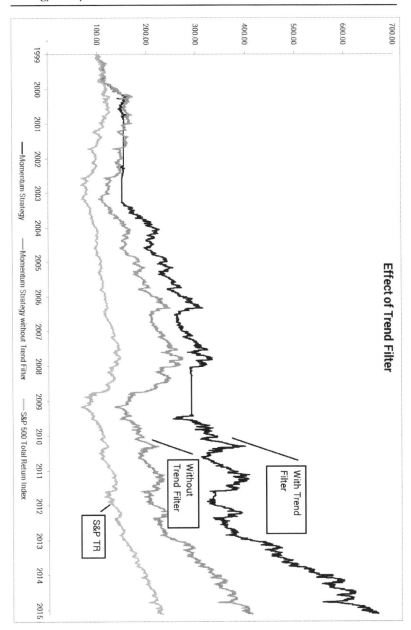

Figure 14-1 Effect of Trend Filter

Table 14-1 Trend Filter Comparison

	Momentum Strategy	Momentum Strategy without Trend Filter	S&P 500 Total Return Index
Annualized Return	12.4%	9.1%	5.2%
Maximum Drawdown	-24.3%	-50.9%	-55.3%

If you run an optimization, you may come to the conclusion that a moving average of 237 days or 178 days works best. That might make you actually believe that this has any bearing on the future. All you have is a curve fitted result to a specific historical series. What you need to do is to think in terms of concepts, not in exact numbers.

If you optimize further, perhaps you'll find that years divisible by 3 should have a different trend filter speed than years where the there's a lunar eclipse. That doesn't necessarily help you trade in the future.

Avoid the urge to optimize. Trade concepts instead. You need a long term trend filter of some sort. How you make it isn't very important.

How important is Risk Parity?

Very.

Do you want to know an easy way to beat the index? Use risk parity sizing instead of market cap weighting. Done.

Let's take a step back and look at the S&P Index again and how it's composed. This is the US large cap index and it contains the most valuable 500 companies in the US. The term valuable refers to the, quite theoretical, value that the whole company has, called market capitalization. You can calculate this value by checking how many shares a company has issued and multiply that by the current stock price. It changes by the second when the stock exchange is open, every time a trade is made. The value of a company is of course something highly theoretical, as you couldn't really buy the whole company by coughing up this theoretical value.

The S&P 500 Index uses the value of the company, the market capitalization or simply market cap, as the basis for weights. The most valuable company gets the highest weight. All the weights are in proportion to their values. This means that the index will inevitably be driven primarily by the largest companies and that the smaller stocks don't really have much impact.

This type of weighting makes a lot of sense for an index. The point of an index after all is to be able to gauge the overall market. As such, the S&P methodology is just fine. It's certainly better than the archaic price weighting that the Dow uses.

Even though the market cap weighting is fine for the index, that doesn't mean that it's a rational way to invest. What would be the reason for buying 4% Apple but only 0.01% of Diamond Offshore Drilling? Is Apple really 400 times better somehow? Diamond has a market cap of over 4 billion, so it's not exactly a little penny stock either.

More importantly, what are the potentials for the world's largest stocks to double? To triple? When a stock has a market cap of 750 billion dollars, twice of the world's second largest company, how likely is it that it will go to 1.5 trillion dollars? Is there really enough potential in such a stock to warrant 400 times the size of the smaller stocks? Can't we come up with a better way to invest in the US large cap stocks? And can we please stop asking questions now?

Enter risk parity. Remember how we calculated risk parity sizing back in chapter 8. The concept is to measure past volatility and assign position weight inverted to that. It's easier than it may sound. What we want to accomplish is that very volatile stocks get a smaller allocation while the slow moving stocks get a larger allocation. Thereby every stock has an equal, theoretical possibility to impact the portfolio level results. Because let's face it, at a weight of 0.01%, Diamond Offshore is pretty much out of luck when it comes to voting how the S&P moves.

The simulation here is simple in concept, as most worthwhile simulations tend to be. We buy all the index stocks, all 500 of them. Each stock is allocated a weight based on its inverse volatility. No, that's not complex. Higher vola, lower weight.

Each month, we check the volatility of all stocks and adjust the weights accordingly. This kind of rebalancing is very important, as we'd otherwise be left with a completely random portfolio. Risks change over time, and we need to change positioning with it.

When a stock leaves or joins the index, the same rebalance is triggered to make sure we're always holding the actual constituents at any given point in time.

Yes, that's an absolutely massive outperformance in Figure 14-2. This is quite a well-known phenomenon in the business, that smaller stocks tend to perform better over time. Still, we did have a loss of about half during 2008, which is in-line with the index. Losing this much isn't fun and that can be avoided with a trend filter as we've seen before.

You may be wondering why we bother with the momentum stock selection. Why not just slap an index trend filter on this baby and let it rip?

It probably works, in theory. For most people however, holding a portfolio of 500 stocks may be a little impractical. Simply by using a risk parity weighting, we can realize a large part of the momentum effect, but it's not a practical solution for most investors. That's why we attempt to build a small portfolio of the top performing stocks.

Table 14-2 Risk Parity Index Weighting

	All Index Stocks, Risk Parity	S&P 500 Total Return Index
Annualized Return	13.1%	5.2%
Maximum Drawdown	-48.4%	-55.3%

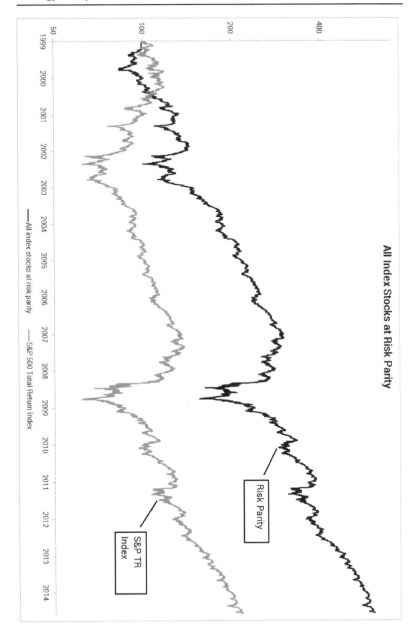

Figure 14-2 All Index Stocks, Risk Parity Weighting

How important is Momentum Period?

In the simulations earlier, we've been using a 90 day momentum ranking. This refers to the number of data points used to calculate the regression analytic that we've seen previously. We measure the momentum based on the past 90 trading days and use that to rank the stocks. But why 90 days?

The short answer is, because it's good enough. If you stay in the more or less medium term momentum range, it doesn't matter that much what exact number you pick.

Running optimizations is rarely a good idea. Perhaps if I ran a few hundred iterations, I'll come up with that 97, 74, 103 or some other number is optimal. Those exercises do little but to lull you into a false sense of safety. After all, it's not terribly likely that there is such a thing as an optimal number. Curve fitting history is easy but it doesn't help you. What you need to do is to trade a concept, not a magical number. Here we're aiming for medium term, so a reasonable medium term number was picked more or less at random.

Sanity checking however is a different thing and shouldn't be confused with optimizations. An easy way to do a rough sanity check is to pick a few more possible numbers that are also reasonable in this context. Then we'll make sure that we get a very similar behavior. If we would get a substantial difference in results, the overall concept wouldn't appear very stable. What we'd like to see is that varying the inputs a bit doesn't make a huge amount of difference.

Since we used 90 before, let's throw a few similar numbers at the wall and see what sticks. The exact same simulation has been repeated a few times, using the periods 60, 120 and 240. Table 14-3 shows the result.

Table 14-3 Regression Period Stability

	60 days	90 days	120 days	240 days
Annualized Return	10.8%	12.3%	12.5%	11.6%
Maximum Drawdown	-28.3%	-24.0%	-24.6%	-26.3%

As can be seen, 90 days seems like a reasonable choice. We see a little worse results if we move down to 60 days, but we're still strongly beating the index. Going up to 120 days shows almost exactly the same results and 240 days only worsens the results slightly. Most likely, any of these numbers would do just fine in the long run.

The exact number you pick isn't of very high importance.

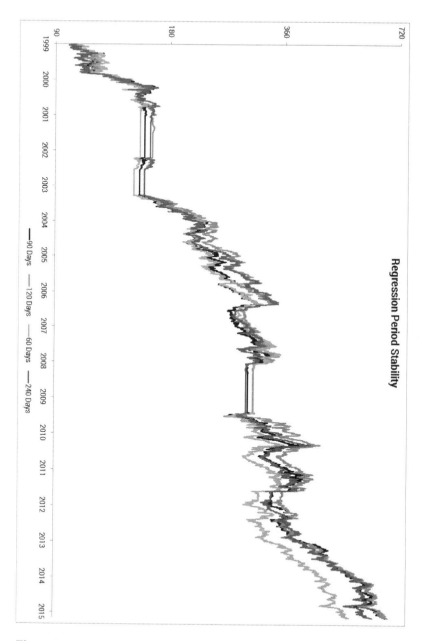

Figure 14-3 Regression Period Stability

How important is Ranking Methodology?

I've shown you a ranking methodology here that I like. It may seem complex if you're not familiar with statistical analysis, but it's really not very difficult math. You may rightly be wondering why I'm describing such a seemingly complex method.

To keep you from flipping the pages back to chapter 7, let me remind you that the ranking math described previously is based on annualized exponential regression, multiplied by the coefficient of determination. Well, that last sentence was a mouthful, huh. Trust me, it sounds more complicated than it is.

I've described this method to you because I like it. It will provide candidate stocks that look comfortable to me. The annualized exponential regression is a useful measurement of pure momentum, expressed in a way that's easy to relate to. It tells you how many percent the stock would move if it continues the same exact trajectory for a full year. It does not however tell you anything about volatility. So we punish volatile stocks by multiplying with the coefficient of determination (R^2). That pushes volatile stocks, prone to gaps and choppy moves, much further down the list. In the end, we get stocks with nice, smooth return profiles.

If you were to simplify my model and use easier measurements, it's not going to make a huge difference. If you have another way to measure the same thing, go ahead and do that. Make sure you get the concept and that whatever methodology you prefer to use covers the same principles. You probably want to measure momentum and reward stocks that move up more smoothly than others.

But what if we were to simplify things a bit? Let's do some simpler models and see what comes out. Redoing the same simulations with simpler momentum measurements could help illustrate why I've chosen the method presented earlier.

Let's look at two simpler ways of measuring momentum. One obvious way would be to simply look at percent covered. Using the same 90 day period as before, we would then measure how many percent a stock made or lost in the past 90 trading days and make ranking tables based on that. Let's use that as one alternative ranking method.

Then there's the matter of using this coefficient of determination business to adjust for fitness. Let's take that away, using just the annualized regression slope, based on 90 trading days, and see what we get.

With these two simpler methods, we can make new simulations and compare the results.

Table 14-4 Different Ranking Methods

	Annualized Regression multiplied by R2	Pure Percent	Pure Regression
Annualized Return	12.4%	12.7%	12.9%
Maximum Drawdown	-24.3%	-26.2%	-24.1%

Table 14-4 seems to show that there's really not much difference. If you look at the chart in Figure 14-4 it still doesn't look like much of a difference. In fact, just looking at that chart it may seem as if the simpler methods are superior. After all, they do land slightly higher on the y-axis.

Well, first of all, the tiny difference in performance merely amounts to a rounding error. Such small differences in simulation results are really nothing but noise. So let's call them all the same in terms of performance.

If they are the same, then why use a complex method?

It's not just about the end result. It's about how you get there and your ability to get there. While the end result is practically the same, the simpler methods will lead you to invest in many dangerous or nonsensical situations. In the long run, it evens out, as long as you really follow the rules. If you're not comfortable with the stocks that the system spits out however, you're unlikely to keep buying them.

The fitness adjusted regression method that I present in this book is designed to find solid momentum situations and to weed out the dangerous and uncomfortable situations. It won't lead you to invest in takeover situations. It won't make you buy stocks that just had a massive one time jump. It will come up with stocks that look good, that make sense and that you won't have any problem buying.

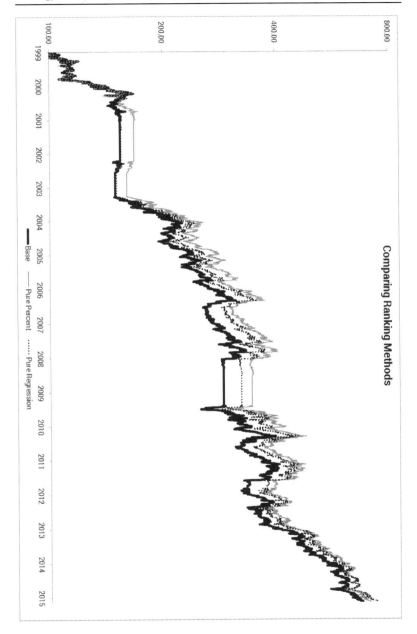

Figure 14-4 Comparing Ranking Methods

How important is Position Size?

Do you remember how we sized the positions earlier? You should, because the principle behind it is pretty important. What we did was to look at the volatility for each stock and buy less of the volatile stocks and more of the slow moving stocks. The idea is to take approximately equal risk per stock. That part is very important. But how much risk should we take per stock?

Remember that in our original formula, explained in chapter 8 we used a risk factor of 10 basis points. This risk factor isn't about the total risk in the portfolio, but only about the risk per stock. We still buy stocks until we run out of cash. If we were to lower the risk factor, each position would be smaller. That would of course mean that we end up with a higher number of stocks in the portfolio. Conversely, if we raise the risk factor we get fewer but larger positions.

So why did we use the number 10 basis points in that first version? Is there something special about that number? Nah, not really. But it's a reasonable enough number. With that number, you normally end up with somewhere between 20 and 30 stocks in a fully loaded portfolio. The exact number will of course depend on how volatile stocks you picked, based on the ranking method.

A portfolio of 20 to 30 stocks makes for a reasonable diversification. If you have really few stocks, you've got too high event risk. In a portfolio of less than 10 stocks, the risk of a shock event in one stock is too high. Sure, it can happen in either direction but it still introduces an element of luck to the strategy. A sudden shock in one stock can make or break your whole year in such a concentrated portfolio.

On the other hand, if you've got too many stocks you're got a different set of problems. It's not really practical for most people to have 50 stocks in a portfolio. You'll also end up with results that are increasingly starting to look like the index.

Having pointed out these issues and explained why I picked 10 basis points, let's see what the simulations will tell us.

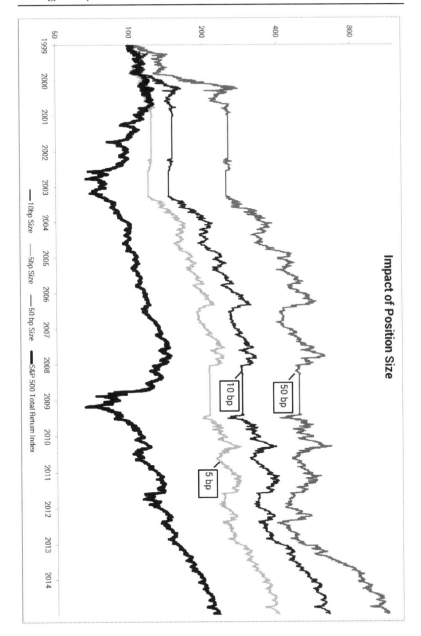

Figure 14-5 The Impact of Position Size

In Figure 14-5 you can compare the results of different position sizes. At the bottom in that figure is the index itself. All of our iterations beat the index. The three simulations shown here use the default 10 basis points, 50 basis points and 5 basis points respectively. Using 5 basis points will generate a very broad portfolio with many stocks, while 50 basis points will hold only 5-6 stocks at any given time.

Table 14-5 Impact of Position Size

	10bp Size	5bp Size	50 bp Size	S&P 500 Total Return Index
Annualized Return	12.3%	9.0%	16.3%	5.2%
Maximum Drawdown	-23.8%	-20.4%	-40.3%	-55.3%

The interesting thing here is that in the simulations, the results look stronger the larger the positions are. Now keep in mind that we're not talking about taking on higher overall exposure, simply about buying larger, and fewer positions.

So isn't the conclusion that you should have an extremely narrow portfolio? Perhaps only 3-4 stocks? Well, I wouldn't recommend it. In theory, such a portfolio can do extremely well over time. It can also be the victim of plain bad luck and crash badly.

Don't lose perspective of what we're doing here and what effect we're trying to exploit. If we have only 3-4 stocks, or even 8-10 stocks the event risk is far too high. Simulations show that it probably works well over longer term, but it's not a prudent way of managing money. The dependency on luck becomes too large.

And what about the really broad portfolio version? Using 5 basis points per stock, we'll end up with 40-50 stocks and often even more. Not only do the simulations show that the results worsen, but it also becomes much more difficult to manage from a practical point of view.

An advantage of stocks compared to futures for instance is that you can trade with much smaller amounts. The default version with 10 basis points and 20-25 stocks can be implemented with a very low capital base. However, if you're targeting a portfolio of 40 stocks, you'd end up buying single shares of each and you'll lose the effect of risk parity and rebalancing.

So is 10 basis points the perfect number? Of course not, but it's a sane number that's probably good enough. Whether you use 8 or 15 will probably have a very marginal impact, but you'd want to be somewhere in this vicinity.

How important is Choice of Index?

The choice of index will over time have quite a large effect. If this book managed to get you interested enough in the subject to start doing your own research, this is an area where you may want to do some work.

When writing a book, some simplifications and limitations are necessary. Covering everything would make for a too lengthy book, would take too long to write and would probably end up too boring for most readers. One simplification in this book is that it focuses on a single index: The S&P 500.

The choice of S&P 500 index is simply realism. It's an index everyone knows about. Most people are invested in it, one way or another. It consists of the 500 largest companies in the largest economy in the world. It's certainly not chosen because momentum somehow works better on this particular index.

A large part of momentum portfolio strategies is about picking up stocks with significant potential. The large cap stocks in the S&P 500 are in this particular index because they had huge potential in the past and have become valuable enough to be included in this index. While these stocks can certainly still show some performance, they are unlikely to have as much potential as they did in the past. Before they were large caps.

The momentum approach doesn't work on the S&P 500 stocks because they are large caps. It works in spite of the stocks being large caps.

If you really want to put in some work and do some serious research, try other indexes. Start with the S&P 400 mid-cap index and the S&P 600 small-cap index. Try local country indexes in other nations or try international indexes. Just remember that if you're using an index with multiple currencies, you need to handle the currency conversions and attributions.

What you're likely to find is that small to medium sized stocks can show an even greater momentum potential than what we've seen in this book. They may also show more volatile returns of course.

15
A Random Ass kicking of Wall Street

If all you want to do is to beat the index, you don't need any of what you've just read so far in this book. Would you like to learn how to beat practically all mutual fund managers in the world? Yep, I'm about to share that secret with you.

Let's first put the whole index beating game into context. There are thousands of mutual funds. Many thousands. Banks all around the world have their own set of mutual funds on just about any index you can dig up. The idea with a mutual fund is, or at least was, to allow individuals with limited net worth to participate in the broad equity markets. It's difficult for a private person of normal background to buy all 500 stocks in the S&P 500 index, but with mutual funds he could buy a fund that will follow and attempt to outperform it.

Mutual funds can't run around and do whatever they please. They have strict tracking error budgets and are not allowed to deviate much from the index composition. Outperforming by 100 basis points in a year, and that's a single percent, is considered a very strong year. It's important to remember that mutual funds are relative investment vehicles. Their job isn't to make money per se, their job is to attempt to beat the benchmark. That's done by investing in a very similar manner and using the tiny tracking error budget to try to make up for the added layers of cost that a mutual fund has.

A mutual fund is not tasked with showing absolute return. If its benchmark index ends a year at -10%, the mutual fund isn't supposed to be positive. If that funds ends the year at -9.5%, that's a successful results in the context of its mission. It's all about the relative performance.

What we saw in chapter 2 was that almost all mutual funds fail dramatically at the single task that they're supposed to focus on.

Typically 75-85% of mutual funds underperform on any given 3 year period. If you look at any longer period than that, there are practically no funds left that managed to even match the index. So why do mutual fund managers fail to beat the S&P 500? According to Gordon Gekko, because they're sheep, and sheep get slaughtered. More likely because they're handcuffed to a tracking error system. They need to keep their allocation very close to the index. For them it's a disaster if they underperform with a couple of percent in a year. Then add in that they have huge costs to pay. Management fees, custody fees, trading fees etc.

If you really want the index, there's of course a solution. Buy the ETF. If you want to get the exact performance of the S&P 500, minus a tiny fee, buy the SPY tracker. It's invested in the exact same stocks as the index, at the exact same weights. When you buy the tracker, a computer will increase holdings pro rata in all stocks automagically. You know in advance exactly what you'll get. You buy the index, and you'll get the index.

But do you really want the index?

The S&P 500 Trading System

The S&P 500, along with all other market indexes, is just a trading system. There are rules for when to buy and when to sell. There are rules for how much to buy from each stock and there are even rules about rebalancing. The S&P 500 is a very long term trading system with extended holding periods. Stocks are bought after strong performance has pushed their market capitalization over a certain limit and certain other criteria have been fulfilled. The position sizing is based on the market capitalization and the higher market cap gets the highest weight.

It may seem strange to think of the S&P 500 as a trading system, but that's what it really is. This also means that we should be able to analyze it like any other trading system.

If you think of things that way, the index doesn't look very attractive anymore. It's a horrible trading system. In the long run you can expect an annualized return of 5 to 6%, while you'll see plenty of huge losses along the way. At times even losing half of your money with several years to recover losses.

So even though you could buy the SPY index tracker and get almost exactly the same performance as the index, beating all the mutual funds, it's still not a very attractive investment. We need to beat the index.

Beating the index must be very hard. After all, all of these professional mutual fund managers keep failing year after year. They're experienced market professionals, making millions of dollars in bonuses. If they can't beat the market, can it really be done?

Oh yes.

Beating the market is very simple. Super simple. A random number generator can beat the index.

I'm serious. Random stocks will beat the index. Big time.

Let's see what some simple simulations can tell us about beating the index. We'll build random portfolios and see what happens.

In the following simulation, we'll let the computer pick stocks from the S&P 500 constituents at random. At the start of every month, we liquidate the entire portfolio and buy 50 random stocks. The position sizing is done through a basic risk parity model. That is, we use the same simple ATR based model as was outlined in chapter 8 to allocate an approximate equal risk to each stock. We have no idea which stock will perform and which will not, so there's no need to allocate different risk to them. Certainly there's no need to allocate a higher risk just because the company happens to be larger.

This being a random approach, a single simulation run wouldn't mean much of course. After all, if you throw the dice once, you could get any value. I've run the simple simulation model a few hundred times and the results in the end are fairly consistent. Not a single iteration has failed to beat the index.

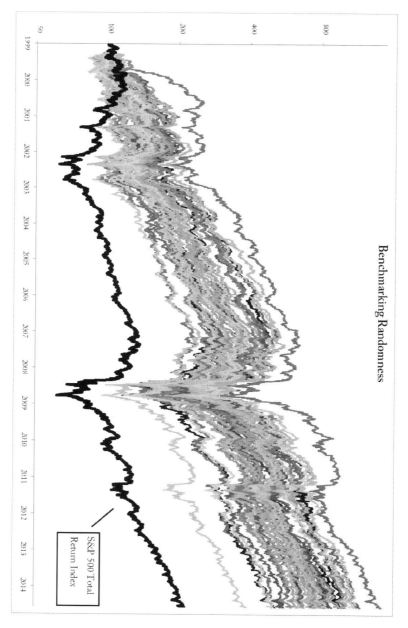

Figure 15-1 Benchmarking Randomness

Figure 15-1 shows a representative subset of 50 simulation runs versus the total return index. The thick black line is the S&P 500 Total Return. Why only a subset of 50 runs? Well, even 50 gets a little silly in a chart. With 500 lines, it would look like something from Picasso's more drug fueled periods.

If you look closer at this figure, you'll see that in the short run, anything can happen. Some months the index may do better, some months the random strategies. There was even a period in the beginning where the index was ahead. In the longer run however, the index doesn't stand a chance.

I'm not seriously suggesting that you go pick a random set of stocks every month. But I'm serious about claiming that if you would, you'd have a high probability of beating the index.

It's important to remember what really differs between this random approach and the momentum approach explained for the better part of this book. First, we try to make sure that we're hitting the stocks in those upper lines in Figure 15-1. We want to increase our probabilities of our returns resembling the better looking of those iterations. Second, we want to avoid or at least reduce the drawdowns. In concept, very easy. In practice, not always as simple.

The real question is, in the light of this random ass kicking of Wall Street, do you really want to buy index products?

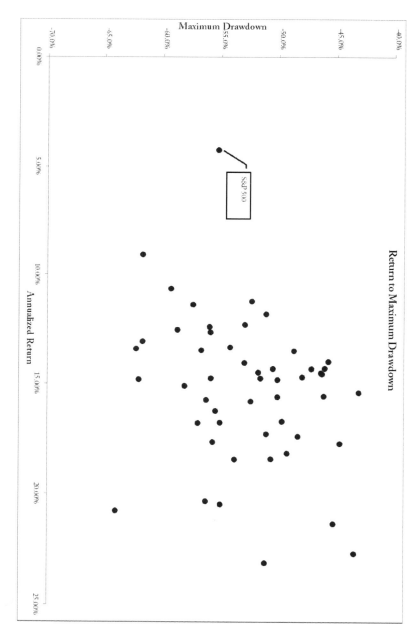

Figure 15-2 Random Victory - Return to Drawdown

16
Simulating the Strategy

As simple as an equity momentum strategy is in terms of concept, it's surprisingly complex to model and simulate it. It's very easy to miss critical details or to make other mistakes along the way. Technology changes all the time so I won't go into software solutions and data providers here. Those types of things are better covered on a website, where the information can be updated as the situation evolves. Instead, this chapter attempts to point out some of the more tricky concepts that can be very important when simulating an equity momentum strategy.

If you accept my simulation results in this book and have no interest in performing your own simulations, you can safely skip this entire chapter.

Data

If you input junk, you'll get junk out. You can make the best simulation in the world, but if you didn't get the data right in the first place it will still be useless. Getting the data right for stock simulations is tricky.

At first, you'll need to figure out what your data universe is. It shouldn't be a basket of stocks that you like. Odds are that you like them because they performed well, so running a simulation of them would probably also show strong results. That's not terribly useful information. What you need is a logical set of markets, something you might have chosen a long time ago.

Picking an index is a rational way to solve this. Trading the constituents of an index makes perfect sense and it's a rule based approach that can be properly tested. In my simulations earlier in this book, I used the S&P 500.

Finding out which stocks are currently part of the S&P 500 is easy, not to mention free. The problem is of course that you can't assume that you would have traded the current S&P 500 stocks for the past ten years. The index changes in composition all the time.

To make matters worse, a stock is usually included because it had very strong price development. So if you run a 10 year momentum stock simulation on the current S&P 500 stocks, of course it's going to look amazing.

You could even argue that the S&P 500, along with most other equity indexes, are already momentum strategies.

No, what you need is to take historical joiners and leavers into account. That is, on any given day in your simulation, your code needs to be aware of which stocks was part of the index on that particular day. That makes it a little trickier, doesn't it?

Did I mention that this includes delisted stocks? Yes, even if a stock went bankrupt five years ago, was merged with another stock or for some other reason ceased to exist, it has to be included. Getting the data for these stocks can be a bit of a hassle and it certainly rules out all the free sources.

Next important point is cash dividends. Over time, this makes a very significant difference. There are two ways to handle the dividend data, once you've found a way to obtain it. Either you use dividend factors calculated by your data provider, to create total return series, or you handle the cash injections directly. Both ways create good enough simulation results.

If you're planning on skipping any of these parts, your simulation work will be a waste of time. You absolutely need to have historical constituents information, delisted stock data and cash dividend data. It can get expensive and it can get complicated, but there's no way around it.

To replicate the strategy in this book, you'll only need end of day data. You won't need any intraday time series, although of course it won't hurt. If you do have intraday series, you can get some interesting stats on the short term moves but it won't improve the strategy as such.

Real Portfolio Simulation

There are several good simulation platforms available. But there are even more absolutely useless software platforms. The latter are usually better known, have a wider user base and considerably lower price points.

Most of the well-known simulation platforms marketed to the retail trading community are based on single strategy, single instrument. This quite outdated concept assumes that you want to simulate a single set of rules on a single market. It's based on the age old illusion of finding the perfect set of rules for trading the NASDAQ. If you list the first ten simulation programs you can think of, odds are that all of them belong in this category.

Single strategy, single market type of software solutions are quite useless for any sort of professional use. Forget about using such software and move on to something that can at least handle portfolios.

The next level is software packages that were built for single instrument, but which has been retrofitted with some sort of portfolio functionality. The products in this group can be a bit hit-and-miss. Some work ok, others are junk. None of them, to my knowledge and experience, are great.

The usual problem is in how they process the data, or rather in which order. The platforms that have been retrofitted with portfolio functionality, rather than having been built for it from the start, tend to process the data in a highly unrealistic manner. This can, and often will, lead to weird results, to use the technical term for it.

Such solutions usually process one instrument at a time. If you tell it to perform a simulation on a set of instruments, it will pick one of them to start with and iterate through every single data point for that instrument before moving on to the next. So if you deal in daily data, it will first go over each day in the data series for Instrument 1 before going over each day for the data series in Instrument 2, and so on.

After going over all instruments in that order, checking for buy and sell points, the common solution is do one more run to determine position sizes.

In reality, you don't trade ten years for Stock 1 and then ten years for Stock 2. Even if the software attempts to figure out some portfolio interaction along the way, it's just not a realistic way to model and it can very easily cause problems. Not the least that it allows for data snooping, i.e. letting your code see into the future.

A proper simulation environment works differently. Instead of working through one instrument at a time, it works through points in time. If you're dealing with daily data, it should look at one day at a time, for all instruments. Your code shouldn't be aware of anything in the future, but it should be aware of everything that's happened up to this point. Those with a programming background reading this know that I'm talking about marshaling. No, I won't go into that word in more detail, because if you're not familiar with it you probably won't need to be. As long as you understand the difference between working though day by day or instrument by instrument.

Programming Language

If you want to be a systematic trader, you will have to learn how to program. It's not something that you can outsource. All too often, this aspect of the job is glossed over. Even if you're head of a team of hedge fund quants, you still need to understand programming.

There was a time when a doctor or a lawyer didn't need to know how to use a typewriter. They had people doing that for them and they were far too busy to be engaged in such menial activities. That's unfortunately how many aspiring traders view programming. Can you imagine today a lawyer who can't type? Of course he's got an assistant, but being unable to type would make him absolutely helpless.

The good news is that you won't need to learn any deeper programming skills. It might be an advantage for some who do want to go deeper, but it's not required. Some basic programming skills however can't be avoided if you want to be in the systematic trading field.

Of course, when I use the word basic in the last sentence, I'm not suggesting that you study how to make Goto statements in Basic. Selecting the right language to build your strategy in can be very important though.

Most retail simulation platforms use simplified, proprietary scripting syntax. The marketing text is usually about how easy it is to get started, even for non-programmers. Avoid these types of programs. They are extremely limited and you can't do anything useful with them.

What you need is flexibility. That's the single most important point when you're deciding about a simulation environment. Speed is not that much of an issue, unless you move to really low frequencies and in that space the larger players have too much of an advantage anyhow.

You won't find flexibility with the simplified scripting languages that are built into many of the retail platforms. You will find it however with industry standard programming languages. You'll also find plenty more support, examples and resources if you use such languages. Whether you want to code in C#, R, MatLab or similar is a matter of preference and convenience. You should however aim for a real programming language, and avoid the scripting platforms. It may seem easy and quick to get started with these simplified platforms, but you'll quickly regret it when you realize just how limited they are.

Flexibility

Very few simulation platforms can do everything you need. Probably none can. The good ones however, can be made to do it anyhow. A good simulation platform is flexible enough to be extended in ways that the original developer didn't think of. The more open a platform is, the better. As a strategy developer, you'll always run into situations where you wish your platform could do something more. That's also a key reason why industry standard languages are important.

For instance, there are probably no simulation platforms that were made with our type of strategy in mind. After all, we're doing something quite different from what most people are simulating. We're calculating analytics, ranking stocks, selecting stocks based on the ranking and sizing them based on both their own volatility and on current overall portfolio value. That's not your everyday simulation.

We might also be interested in data such as sector attribution or portfolio allocation on a given date back in time. Perhaps we want to analyze industry risk and attribution over time or the impact of the positive and negative stock outliers. A good platform is able to do all of those things, with a little work. If it's flexible enough.

Multi-Currency Support

You may have noticed that I've deliberately kept currencies out of the discussions so far. The strategy we've seen so far has only been applied on American stocks. That's not because they somehow work better with momentum strategies. It's not even about how it's easier to sell a book about American stocks than about Swiss stocks. Well, not only about that. It's because I'd assume that most people who want to replicate the strategy lack access to multi-currency simulation environments.

Dealing in stocks denominated in only one single currency is a luxury. If you've ever managed global portfolios and go back to single currency portfolios, it feels like vacation time. No more currency exposure problems!

When you've got a stock universe covering several currencies, you will be faced with a whole new set of problems. There are many practical considerations, decisions such as if, how and when to cover exposure, added costs in terms of foreign exchange spreads and the pesky little issue of currency attribution. It opens up a whole new type of headaches in practice, but even on the simulation stage it makes things much more complicated.

When you simulate such strategies, it's vital that your software is aware of the currency denominations of your stocks as well as the exchange rate at any given time. The currency fluctuations will have a very large impact on your performance. If you plan to hedge your exposure, you'd have to model that hedging strategy too. That would require capability to model and simulate multiple strategies of course.

Or you could stick to the S&P 500 stocks for an easy way to get rid of this problem.

Structuring the Simulation

For each day in your simulation, you need to check or calculate a few things.

First you need to check if the stock qualifies for inclusion or not. In this case, we check if the stock was a member of the S&P 500 index on the day in question. A convenient way to do this is to construct a custom indicator, which uses reference data to return 1 on days when a stock was in the index in question and 0 when it wasn't.

Then we need to calculate the largest move that the stock did in the past 90 days. Remember how we had that rule that we don't like stocks that had gaps larger than 15%? Calculate how large gap we've seen in the past 90 days for use later.

Of course, we need a crude volatility measurement and for that the Average True Range is a good choice. We'll use a 20 day ATR in the base version of this strategy, so add that into the mix.

Then comes the ranking itself. That is, the analytic that we use to select which stocks to trade. We therefore need an indicator that tells us the risk adjusted momentum. The math isn't terribly complicated if you're familiar with statistics. You need to first calculate the annualized exponential regression slope, based on 90 days, and then multiplying it by the correlation of determination (R^2).

The ranking is explained earlier in chapter 7.

Apart from the information mentioned above, we also need to calculate a 200 day moving average on the index itself, and determine whether or not it's currently higher or lower than the index itself.

Once all the data mentioned above is calculated, we can start performing the logic. The first thing you need to do now is to rank the stocks. Use the ranking number we calculated, make a list of all the stocks that qualify on this particular day and sort them based on the ranking number we calculated.

Note that this process so far aims to replicate what we would do in reality. We calculate all the relevant analytics at the end of the day and then we take action based on it.

The logic is only performed once per week. The lazy solution to this is to run the simulation on weekly data. The better way would be to check for which day the logic should be done. If you go down to weekly periodicity, you'll lose the granularity on the simulation results as well and that's a big loss.

If today is a trading day, we start by checking if we need to sell anything. If a stock that we own left the index or for other reasons stopped trading, exit it. If the momentum rank is no longer in the top 100, exit. If the stock is trading below its 100 day moving average, exit it. If it had a gap larger than 15%, exit.

Next step is to check if today is a rebalancing day. If so, we need to go over each position, calculate how large size we should have and what the difference is to what we have. Remember the rules and how we size the positions, as explained in chapter 8. Recalculate the size using the same formula and adjust the position size up or down as needed to match. To reduce trading a little, you could set a filter to only adjust if the difference is larger than 5%.

Now that we've sold the stocks we no longer want and rebalanced the ones we want to keep, we know how much cash is available. That's when we can start buying.

Start from the top of the ranking list. Buy from the top, using the same risk parity sizing as before, until you run out of cash. If a stock is top ranked and we don't yet own it, buy it.

That's it.

Did I hear anyone ask for source code? Well, that's not as useful as it may seem. You're better off understanding the logical steps and building it yourself. My source code is written in a particular language for a particular environment and it's probably not in itself too useful for most readers.

If you really want to get into the simulation side, you've got some hard work in front of you. I do very much encourage you to do so, but you're going to have to do some heavy lifting.

With the logic I've explained here, along with quality data and a proper simulation environment, you will be able to replicate my findings and experiment with your own improvements. That's not for everyone, but with this chapter I want to give everyone who is interested enough information to get to work.

I wish you the best of luck and hope to see many new successful momentum investors!

17
Bibliography

Antonacci, G. (2014). *Dual Momentum Investing: An Innovative Strategy for Higher Returns with Lower Risk*. McGraw-Hill.

Clenow, A. F. (2013). *Following the Trend: Diversified Managed Futures Trading*. Wiley.

https://us.spindices.com/resource-center/thought-leadership/spiva/. (n.d.). Retrieved from S&P Dow Jones SPIVA Scorecards: https://us.spindices.com/resource-center/thought-leadership/spiva/

Jegadeesh, N., & Titman, S. (1993). *Return to Buying Winner and Selling Losers: Implications for Stock Market Efficiency*. Blackwell Publishing.

Kaminski, K. M., & Greyserman, A. (2014). *Trend Following with Managed Futures*. Wiley.

Levy, R. A. (1967). *Relative Strength as a Criterion for Investment Selection*. Journal of Finance.

Radge, N. (2012). *Unholy Grails: A New Road to Wealth*. Radge Publishing.

Wilcox, C., & Crittenden, E. (2005). *Does Trend Following Work on Stocks*. Longboard Asset Management.

Winton Capital Management. (2015). *The Global Monkey*.

Made in the USA
Middletown, DE
16 July 2024

57364542R00159